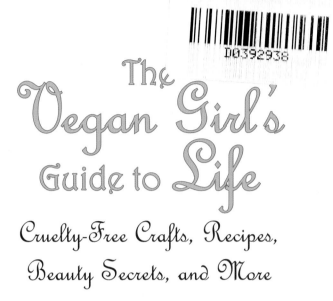

The Vegan Girl's Guide to Life

Cruelty-Free Crafts, Recipes, Beauty Secrets, and More

Melisser Elliott

Skyhorse Publishing

Skyhorse Publishing books may be purchased in bulk at special discounts for sales promotion, corporate gifts, fund-raising, or educational purposes. Special editions can also be created to specifications. For details, contact the Special Sales Department, Skyhorse Publishing, 555 Eighth Avenue, Suite 903, New York, NY 10018 or info@skyhorsepublishing.com.

www.skyhorsepublishing.com

10 9 8 7 6 5 4 3 2 1

Library of Congress Cataloging-in-Publication Data

Elliott, Melisser.
The vegan girl's guide to life : cruelty-free crafts, recipes, beauty secrets, and more / by Melisser Elliott.
        p. cm.
ISBN 978-1-61608-092-1 (pbk. : alk. paper)
1. Veganism. 2. Vegans. 3. Women--Health and hygiene. I. Title.
TX392.E476 2010
641.5'636--dc22
        2010028107

Printed in China

CONTENTS

INTRODUCTION

Hi, my name is Melisser, and I am vegan. You may wonder how I came to find veganism, and I figure there's no better way to tell you than to recount my past and the events that have shaped me into the person I am today.

I grew up the oldest of three children in a working-class family. My mother ran a day-care business in our home, and took on other odd jobs to earn money while still being there to take care of us. My father worked at UPS from age nineteen until he retired, a job he kept for the excellent health benefits, so we could make regular doctor visits and have braces on our teeth. We went to church, we took dance lessons . . . we lived modestly, and my parents worked hard to make sure we never went without.

When I think back to my childhood, I realize that I have always been surrounded by animals. No, not my family members, but the cuddly, loving, nonhuman animals many people call pets. At a very young age, I named my first cat, a scrappy orange tabby, Garfield, and he stayed by my side until I was in high school. Garfield was hardly our only feline; because of my mother's affection for animals, our house was the drop-off location for unwanted pets. We often found ourselves with well over ten cats at a time. They all had their own unique personalities: from everyone's favorite tomcat, Kirby, to fluffy Persian princess, Lady Ashley; from the feral calico turned lap cat, Egypt, to Rascal, the one-eyed lover with the scratchy meow.

Because I was good at convincing my mother to let me bring home many new animal companions, we also had rabbits, guinea pigs, rats, hamsters, and birds. As a feral cat colony developed in our neighborhood, my mom and I worked to trap and release the cats, although most of the cats were added to our own family. From the day I was born, I was raised to love and respect animals, and it's something I've kept with me always.

Like most people, I grew up on the standard American diet of meat and potatoes; rarely did a meatless meal appear on our table. Processed food was the norm, with no attention paid to ingredients. This was not through any lack of care on my mother's part; we were all physically fit and seemed to be fine.

At age thirteen I entered high school, where I met a group of vegetarians. I soon decided to become a vegetarian as well. My love for animals was already ingrained in me, and I could no longer fathom eating something I loved. I was your standard junk-food vegetarian: Taco Bell burritos, McDonald's cheeseburgers with no meat, and anything in fried-potato form, especially Tater Tots. My parents weren't exactly thrilled, and I was not allowed to cook on my own, so my meals often consisted of side dishes, which I would supplement with lots of ice cream. Of course, I started to gain weight, but I didn't care, and continued being a junk-food vegetarian, if only for the animals' sake.

I found punk rock, then ska, and started attending shows and meeting like-minded people where I learned about alternative culture, a far cry from my religious upbringing. Music became a crucial part of my life, and I went to as many live shows as possible, often claiming I was spending the night at a friend's house, when I was actually dancing front and center at a music venue.

At seventeen, I was introduced to a guy named Ryan who had been trying to track me down after seeing me at a Hepcat show. It turns out that this was not just any guy, but the one I was destined to marry. We fell in love fast, and by the time I was eighteen, we were living together in San Francisco, with far too many roommates. Like most girls of eighteen, I was a bit insecure and didn't want to be a nuisance, so I slowly incorporated meat back into my diet. I felt horrible and guilty, but we didn't have much money, and I assumed I didn't have other options. I suppressed my feelings about animals and went back to the processed and fast-food American diet of my upbringing.

A few years later I reached my breaking point. I couldn't do it anymore. I couldn't eat the flesh of innocent beings while lavishing affection on my own two cats, Beamish and Scurvy. One night at a Morrissey concert at the London Palladium, I was handed a postcard with a photo of Morrissey standing by a billboard, saying, "I want you to go vegetarian." So I did. I returned to vegetarianism, right then and there. When I told my husband, he was 100 percent supportive. We discussed a "vegetarian household" rule and he obliged, even though he didn't become a vegetarian himself at this time. His choice to eat meat was something he could do on his own time, so he didn't eat it in front of me either, especially since I made most of our meals. All in all, it was an easy transition.

After a trip to New York during the cupcake craze, I tried the baked goods at Magnolia Bakery, and the experience inspired me to try my hand at baking. Up to that point, my idea of making dinner was preparing macaroni and cheese or Pasta Roni, and if I wanted cookies, I went to the supermarket. This new attempt at baking was a success, and it led me to food blogs where I devoured recipes and made new friends.

I noticed a plethora of vegan blogs out there and started reading them, finding my interest piqued about this cruelty-free lifestyle. I tried my hand at vegan baking for a friend's birthday, but it was a failure; how could I go vegan without my beloved baking? As I read more, however, and learned about the cruelty of the dairy industry, and how many cheeses contain rennet from a cow's stomach and aren't even vegetarian, I knew I needed to take the next step and go vegan. I started to gradually make the transition, first cutting out all non-vegan savory foods, and baking an occasional non-vegan dessert. Shortly thereafter I achieved some success with vegan baking, so I went 100 percent vegan. Once again a household rule was discussed, and our "vegan household" was established. It was at this time that my husband Ryan decided to go vegetarian and the dairy got the boot from our house!

During this time I started my blog, The Urban Housewife, and found support from vegans all over the world. From creating a vegan candy-corn recipe to my first international trip as a vegan, it's been a fun ride! About a year after my transition to veganism, Ryan decided to join me and go vegan as well, without any pressure or cajoling from me. Can I say how proud I am here? I mean, seriously, so happy and so proud!

My life story so far wouldn't be complete without mentioning my little dog, Strummer. The day before Father's Day in 2008, Ryan and I were walking to my favorite store, Rainbow Grocery Cooperative, and I saw two guys with the tiniest dog ever. I couldn't help but comment on how adorable this pint-size pup was, and the next thing I knew, I was being asked if I'd like to take her. They claimed to have found her on the sidewalk, and they wanted me to take her off their hands. Never one to leave an animal behind, we walked away with a shivering, flea-ridden, hungry, one-and-a-half-pound Chihuahua puppy.

Over the next few weeks, we checked the area for lost-dog signs and watched craigslist for ads, but no one claimed her. Of course, at this point she was already in puppy classes, had all her shots, and was thriving on a vegan diet, so as far as we were concerned, she was ours!

These days you'll find me peacefully coexisting with my husband, our dog, two cats, and any other living being that enters these doors. I try to take time every day to speak out for the animals, whether it's through leafleting, writing letters, or just sharing the benefits of veganism with others. Going vegan has been a wonderful influence in my life that has made me care more about the world around me, given me new friends in all corners of the globe, and brought me to a new level of consciousness. Sure, it's not all kittens and rainbows, but the positives outweigh the negatives, and I feel good knowing that I'm doing my part to make this a better world.

I hope that this book is a useful resource for you. It contains facts, but it also contains opinions; it's not meant to be the end all, be all of veganism. Whether you are an aspiring vegan or have already taken the plunge toward a cruelty-free lifestyle, you'll find helpful tips and resources contained in these pages.

To my Nana, who gave me my sweet tooth and joy for baking,
and supported me with love and kindness in everything I wanted to do—
even when I wanted to marry Steve Urkel.

The word *veganism* denotes a philosophy and way of living which seeks to exclude—as far as is possible and practical—all forms of exploitation of, and cruelty to, animals for food, clothing or any other purpose; and by extension, promotes the development and use of animal-free alternatives for the benefit of humans, animals and the environment. In dietary terms it denotes the practice of dispensing with all products derived wholly or partly from animals.
—The Vegan Society

CHAPTER 1

UNDERSTANDING WHAT VEGAN IS (AND ISN'T)

In the simplest terms, vegans refrain from the use of all animal products, in diet and lifestyle. This means vegans do not consume meat, dairy, eggs, honey, and their by-products; and vegans do not wear leather, wool, silk, down, or any other animal material that is not suitable for consumption or use by vegans. While this may seem like a lot to avoid, it's far less than what vegans *can* consume. A plentiful variety of vegetables, fruits, grains, legumes, nuts, and seeds is all on the menu, with an abundance of familiar foods from all over the world falling into these categories. There is also a plethora of materials you can wear, products you can use, and things you can do as a vegan, all of which we'll explore in this book.

There are some people who choose to follow a vegan diet but do not refrain from using other animal products, which involve atrocities committed against animals, such as the harvesting of skins for clothing, or the entrapment of animals for human entertainment at zoos and circuses. Being vegan is so much more than what you can or can't eat; it is an ethical stance against the mistreatment of all animals. More than just a diet, it is truly a lifestyle.

THE HISTORY OF VEGANISM

Vegan Society cofounder Donald Watson coined the term *vegan* in 1944, by combining the first three and last two letters of vegetarian to form "vegan," which he saw as "the beginning and end of vegetarian." Three months after coining the term, he explained in The Vegan Society newsletter that the word should be pronounced, "*veegan*, not *veejan*."

Although veganism was given a name in 1944, this was hardly the first time people chose to eschew animal products. Greek philosopher and mathematician Pythagoras mentioned vegetarianism around 500 BCE, and promoted kinship to animals, saying: "As long as man continues to be the ruthless destroyer of lower living beings he will never know health or peace. For as long as men massacre animals, they will kill each other."

Many religions, including Buddhism, Hinduism, Jainism, and Christianity, have a history of followers who abstain from animal products for spiritual reasons. Jainism in particular has advocated for living beings, promoting nonviolence toward all, including animals and insects. Jains take a vow of *Ahimsa*, meaning to do no harm. Their idea of not harming living creatures certainly includes dietary choices, but Jains will also go to extreme measures to ensure that they are not inadvertently killing living beings. This includes guaranteeing that insects are not killed in the building of a structure or the development of a power source.

Vegetarianism became more popular in the mid-nineteenth century, and vegan societies started popping up in America. An early U.S. vegetarian nondairy cookbook, *Vegetarian Cookery* by Dr. Pietro Rotondi, was published in 1942, and the first vegan cookbook, *The Gar Shu Vegetarian Cookbook*, was published in 1957. Health and wellness was the focus of a vegetarian diet in the 1970s, with health-food stores touted as being "crunchy-granola" popping up all over, accompanied by cookbooks courtesy of the Moosewood Collective.

In 1975 Peter Singer's *Animal Liberation* was published in the United States. Considered by many to be a game-changer, this book makes a clear case for the abolishment of modern animal agricultural practices. In the 1980s and 1990s, the animal rights movement gained attention as more pro-animal organizations were formed. Protests and marches increased in popularity, and events like Fur-Free Friday were created.

Today, veganism continues to increase in popularity with help from the Internet, activist efforts, the media, and the expansion of organic and eco-friendly markets. New products are being created that cater to vegans, and labels are being added to merchandise to denote what is suitable for cruelty-free lifestyles. It's a great time to go vegan! It's easier than ever, and with the state of the world, the health of humans, and animal agriculture in dire straits, veganism is more important than ever. So, what can I say? Go vegan and nobody gets hurt!

Marijke

Location: Hamburg, Germany

Blog: Vegan in the City (no-fairytales.blogspot.com)

Reason You Went Vegan: I was vegetarian for several years because I didn't want animals to die for my food. One day I finally realized how stupid it was to quit meat but not eggs, dairy, leather, etc. I started researching animal products and simply found that none of them are produced without harming an animal.

Favorite Dish to Cook: I like simple food, such as spaghetti bolognese or chili con (soy) carne. I enjoy cooking these meals for meat-eaters and not telling them they're vegan. They never notice—that is, until I do my famous "I fooled you" dance.

Funniest Vegan Moment: One day I was so happily surprised that an IKEA in Berlin had cow-free hot dogs that I opted for two of them. Shortly before biting into one, I got confused by the smell. It turned out I was so blinded by the term "cow-free" that I'd actually ordered *chicken* hot dogs. I gave them to a couple standing behind me and toddled off.

GOING VEGAN FOR ETHICAL AND ANIMAL RIGHTS

Most people would say they love animals, but the reality is, if you're using animals for food, clothing, or entertainment, you're only considering the lives of certain animals, typically those of cats and dogs. The United States alone slaughters over ten billion land animals for food every year, and as more people are exposed to the truths of modern animal agriculture practices, they are shocked by the cruelty shown toward innocent creatures. The first step in stopping these atrocities is to vote with your fork and refrain from participating in cruelty.

The way our society treats animals is disgusting and offensive. Here are some facts about animal cruelty from GoVeg.com. While they may be hard to read, it's crucial that you arm yourself with the reality of animal exploitation so that you can better inform others:

- Animals on factory farms are confined in horrendous conditions. By the thousands, chicken, cows, pigs, and turkeys are stuck in gestation crates, cages, and windowless sheds, never to see the outside world or feel the sun on their backs.

- Ninety-five percent of the animals killed every year are chickens. Hens used for eggs are held in battery cages, with five to eight birds crammed into cages that are just 14 square inches. Due to stress-related aggression, chicks are de-beaked with a burning hot blade, and no painkillers. To keep production levels up, hens live in constant light. Male chicks are worthless to the egg industry, and millions of them are killed every year by being tossed into trash bags to suffocate, or they're thrown into high-speed grinders while they are still alive.

- "Broiler chickens"—the ones raised for their flesh—are drugged and bred to grow large so quickly that their legs and organs can't keep up, making heart attacks, organ failure, and crippling leg deformities common. When they are only six or seven weeks old, they are crammed into cages and trucked to slaughter. At the slaughterhouse, their legs are snapped into shackles, their throats are cut, and they are immersed in scalding hot water to remove their feathers. Because they have no federal legal protection (birds are exempt from the Humane Methods of Slaughter Act), most are still conscious when their throats are cut open, and many are literally scalded to death in the feather-removal tanks after missing the throat cutter.

- In the United States, more than 41 million cows suffer and die for the meat and dairy industries every year. Cattle raised for beef are usually born in one state, fattened in another, and slaughtered in yet another. Many cows die on the way to slaughter, and those who survive are shot in the head with a bolt gun, hung up by their legs, and taken onto the killing floor, where their throats are cut and they are skinned. Some cows remain fully conscious throughout the entire process; according to one slaughterhouse worker, in an interview with *The Washington Post*, "they die piece by piece."

- Cows raised for their milk are repeatedly impregnated using artificial insemination. Calves are generally taken from their mothers within a day of being born. The males are destined for veal crates, and the females are sentenced to the same fate as their mothers. Mother cows on dairy farms can often be seen searching and calling for their calves long after they have been separated. After their calves are taken from them, mother cows are hooked up, several times a day, to machines that take the milk intended for their babies. Using genetic manipulation, powerful hormones, and intensive milking, cows are forced to produce about ten times as much milk as they naturally would. They are pumped full of bovine growth hormone, which contributes to a painful inflammation of the udder known as mastitis. A cow's natural life span is twenty-five years, although cows used by the dairy industry are killed after only four or five years. Dairy cows are turned into soup, companion animal food, or low-grade hamburger meat because their bodies are too "spent" to be used for anything else.

- Male calves are considered a by-product of the dairy industry and are generally taken from their mothers when they are less than one day old. The calves are then put into dark, tiny crates where they are kept almost completely immobilized so that their flesh stays tender. The calves are fed a liquid diet that is low in iron and has little nutritive value in order to make their flesh white. This makes the calves ill, and they frequently suffer from anemia, diarrhea, and pneumonia. Frightened, sick, and alone, these calves are killed after only a few months of life to make veal.

- Pigs are considered smarter than a three-year-old child, and yet, as piglets, they are taken away from their mothers when they are less than one month old. Their tails are removed, some of their teeth are cut off, and they are castrated without any pain relief. They spend their entire lives in overcrowded pens on a tiny slab of filthy concrete. Breeding sows spend their entire lives in gestation crates where they can't even turn around. The pigs give birth and then are forcibly impregnated in a cycle that continues for years until their bodies can no longer produce and they are killed. When sent to slaughter, pigs are forced onto transport trucks that travel for many miles through all weather extremes; many die of heat exhaustion in the summer, or arrive frozen to the inside of the truck in the winter. Additionally, many are still fully conscious when they are immersed in scalding water for hair removal.

- Fish farming has become a billion-dollar industry, and more than 30 percent of all the sea animals consumed each year are now raised on these "farms." Aqua farms can be based on land or in the ocean. Land-based farms raise thousands of fish in ponds, pools, or concrete tanks. Ocean-based aqua farms are situated close to shorelines, and fish in these farms are packed into net or mesh cages. All fish farms are rife with pollution, disease, and suffering, regardless of their location. These farmed fish will spend their entire lives crammed together, constantly bumping against each other and the sides of their grossly overcrowded cage. Conditions on some farms are so horrendous that 40 percent of the fish may die before farmers can kill and package them for food.

- Turkeys make up 4 percent of the birds killed each year. They are killed when they are only five or six months old, and the 300 million turkeys raised and killed for their flesh every year in the United States have no federal legal protection. Thousands of turkeys are crammed into filthy sheds after their beaks and toes are burned off with a hot blade, and no painkillers. Many suffer heart failure or debilitating leg pain, often becoming crippled under the weight of their genetically manipulated and drugged bodies. When the time comes for slaughter, they are thrown into transport trucks, and when they arrive at the slaughterhouse, their throats are cut and their feathers burned off—often while they are still fully conscious.

- Ducks and geese raised for their flesh spend their entire lives crammed in dirty, dark sheds where they suffer from injury and disease and are deprived of everything that is natural to them. Ducks and geese raised for *foie gras* endure the pain of having a pipe shoved down their throats three times daily so that two pounds of grain can be pumped into their stomachs to produce the diseased "fatty liver" that some diners consider a delicacy.

- Shortly after birth, lambs are subjected to two painful mutilations: castration and tail docking. About four million newborn lambs, roughly one in five, die every year within a few days of birth, mostly from disease, exposure, or malnutrition. Current European Union rules allow sheep to travel for fourteen hours without water or a rest stop. They must have a rest period of one hour after a fourteen-hour journey, after which they may be transported for a further fourteen hours.

- Rabbits aren't as common at the factory farm, but there have been experiments in battery systems similar to those of hens. Young rabbits have a high death rate. Female rabbits (called "does") are considered disposable. When a doe can't have seven litters a year anymore, she is slaughtered.

- Zoo animals are kept in enclosures that don't allow them to live their lives in a natural way. No matter how nice zoos try to make the enclosures, they don't compare with the ideal natural habitat. Zoo animals have to spend day after day in the exact same enclosure, making their lives very monotonous. Additionally, certain kinds of animals in zoos or circuses develop behavioral disorders and stereotypical behavior, such as chimps tearing out their own fur as well as that of their young; parrots and swans that are more interested in their keepers than in their own kind; giraffes and camels licking a particular spot of the fence; emus and ostriches pacing along the edge of their enclosure; predators circling their cages; and, finally, elephants rhythmically moving their heads from side to side.

- Circus animals are often trained using physical tactics and intimidation. Activists have obtained footage of animals being beaten with hooks, whips, and chains, being poked and prodded and even burned to force them into submission. Elephants are often kept in chains for as long as twenty-three hours a day, from the time they are babies.

- It takes eighteen red foxes to make one fox-fur coat, and fifty-five minks to make one mink coat. So as not to damage their fur, foxes, raccoons, minks, coyotes, bobcats, lynxes, opossums, beavers, muskrats, otters, and many other fur-bearing animals are killed daily on fur farms by anal and vaginal electrocution, and in the wild by drowning, trapping, or beating.

- As many as 115 million animals are experimented on and killed in laboratories in the United States every year. Most of the experimentation—including pumping chemicals into rats' stomachs, hacking muscle tissue from dogs' thighs, and putting baby monkeys in isolation chambers far from their mothers—is paid for by American taxpayers and consumers. Rodents are not protected under the Animal Welfare Act, which means that the law does not require any accounting for the large numbers of rats used. As a result, there is no way to know conclusively just how many millions suffer and die each year in publicly and privately funded research. Animal experimentation is a multibillion-dollar industry fueled by massive public funding and involving a complex web of corporate, government, and university laboratories, cage and food manufacturers, and animal breeders, dealers, and transporters.

ABOLITIONIST VS. WELFARIST, OR ANIMAL RIGHTS VS. ANIMAL WELFARE

When I went vegan, I wasn't aware that there were different approaches to veganism. I thought we all just wanted to stop animal cruelty, and that was it. As I spent time reading about veganism, I saw the terms *abolitionist* and *welfarist* being thrown around quite a bit, so I decided to do more research. I discovered that it's a hotbed of controversy for some vegans, while others are unaware of the debate and just do their best to live their ethics.

According to Gary L. Francione, American legal scholar and Distinguished Professor of Law, "The abolitionist approach maintains that ethical veganism is a moral baseline; it represents the recognition of the moral personhood of animals and the rejection of the notion that animals are commodities for human use. Ethical veganism is an essential component of a commitment to non-violence."

A *welfarist* can be defined as a person who believes it is morally acceptable for humans to use nonhuman animals, provided that the animals suffer little to no adverse effects, while others see it purely as a term to describe people concerned with the welfare of animals. *New welfarist* is a more-recent term; Francione says that new welfarists "claim to endorse veganism but will not promote it as the baseline of the movement because of the concern that veganism will appear to be too 'radical' for the general public."

Some vegans believe that taking incremental steps, such as passing animal-cruelty laws, is the key to public awareness and moving society toward a vegan lifestyle, while others believe these laws take the guilt out of consuming animal products, make people eat what they believe to be "happy meat," and in the end only cause more animal suffering. Another way to break it down is that those in support of animal rights seek the abolition of all animal use, while animal welfare supporters seek regulation, and may or may not support abolition. It's a controversial topic, but whichever camp you belong to, it is important to live your ethics, avoid the infighting, and promote veganism as a way of life for all.

GOING VEGAN FOR HEALTH AND WELLNESS

Many people turn to a vegan diet in times of need, whether they are fighting heart disease or diabetes, looking to be a more-effective athlete, or just want to attain optimum health. A well-planned vegan diet can be an amazing tool in combating and even reversing disease, according to the Physicians Committee for Responsible Medicine, Dr. John McDougall, Dr. Dean Ornish, and many other health specialists. In the book *The China Study,* T. Colin Campbell and Thomas M. Campbell II conducted the largest study of its kind, spanning twenty years, which showed that diet has startling implications for weight and long-term health. Other great resources on the health benefits of veganism include *Diet for a New America* by John Robbins, and Vegan-Health.org, maintained by Vegan Outreach.

A vegan diet is cholesterol-free and can lower your blood pressure, which means vegans are less likely to have heart attacks or stroke. In their paper, entitled "Position of the American Dietetic Association: Vegetarian Diets," *The Journal of the American Dietetic Association* noted, "[T]he results of an evidence-based review showed that a vegetarian diet is associated with a lower risk of death from ischemic heart disease. Vegetarians also appear to have lower low-density lipoprotein cholesterol levels, lower blood pressure, and lower rates of hypertension and Type 2 diabetes than non-vegetarians. Furthermore, vegetarians tend to have a lower body mass index and lower overall cancer rates."

Natala Constantine is an amazing example of what a vegan diet can do for your health and wellness. Her battle with diabetes and the story of how a plant-based diet affected her life is so inspiring that I knew it had to be shared:

> It was about two years ago that I was faced with the possibility of having part of my leg amputated. It's not really something you want to hear when you are thirty years old, but there I was, sitting in a doctor's office with a really bad infection on my lower right leg, and listening to a doctor explain that it was not looking good. That's what diabetes does, eventually; it causes things like a need for the amputation of limbs, blindness, and many other

Carmen

Location: San Francisco, California

Reason You Went Vegan: Animal suffering was the reason. I was in culinary school starting a horrifying butchery class, when the only vegan in our classroom asked a few of us to go vegan for the length of our butchery class. He invited us to come to his place to hang out and cook some amazing vegan food. We agreed. It was a great experience; I made friends, and ate really delicious food. One day, he made us watch a PETA video, which was really smart of him to do, because that got me in! I went vegan that day and never looked back!

Favorite Dish to Cook: Anything really, but my boyfriend and I make really delicious seitan that fools omnivores, and I love seeing their reaction when they find out that their "meat" is fake!

Favorite "Accidentally Vegan" Treat: I was in Mexico for the first time after becoming veg, and the family and I were going to the beach. On our way there we stopped at a little side market to get snacks, drinks, etc. I was going crazy before I even entered the store, already thinking, "It's a waste of time—I'm not going to find anything," but of course, I did. Fritos Sal y Limon! Yummy vegan chips that only have four ingredients: corn, oil, salt, and lemon! I think that's all I ate for the rest of my vacation in Mexico!

really horrible things. I had tried many remedies and every diet under the sun. I had been to specialists, nutritionists, doctors, and more. I was on twelve or thirteen medications, and I was taking close to 200 units (or more) of insulin per day. Insulin, a growth hormone, was making it almost impossible for me to lose any weight, and I was close to 400 pounds at the time.

Things were not looking up, and I had lost hope. Doctors told me that I might possibly live for another ten years, but even that wasn't certain. When you are a thirty-year-old woman, you are supposed to be doing things like running, hanging out with friends, shopping for a great handbag, decorating a house, and working at an awesome job. Instead, I was fighting for my life, and I was potentially going to leave the man that I adore a widower before he was forty—or I would force him to take care of a brittle diabetic with amputations and blindness. This is not what either of us had signed up for, but it's what I would have to deal with.

It was at one of my darkest moments—a moment so painful that I sat in our living room, sobbing, until I couldn't breathe, contemplating taking my own life—when a ray of hope came my way. I was depressed, had not showered in days, was crying all the time, and it had gotten to the point where people were checking in on me to make sure that I didn't harm myself.

My husband insisted that I get out of the house, so I went to our gym to take a water aerobics class. (Even during the worst points of my illness, I was still working out like a madwoman, sometimes four hours per day, which didn't do me a lot of good.) I decided to get in the water to try to calm down. The instructor, a friend of mine, knew of my condition, and after class asked me if I had ever considered looking at my food as medicine. I wanted to slap her. I was so frustrated that she would suggest something so simplistic while I was paying a thousand dollars per visit to see doctors with BMWs.

That same day, I found myself in the health section of a bookstore looking for yet another book on diabetes. I came across one that claimed it could, through diet, reverse diabetes in thirty days. Of course I thought it was impossible, but I decided to read parts of it if only for the mere absurdity of it all. I was hooked after only a few chapters. The author was describing the same things I had been through with my diabetes and weight problems. I would later pick up **Dr. Neal Barnard's Program for Reversing Diabetes,** a book I recommend for anyone interested in the miraculous effect of diet on diabetes.

The cure they had discovered was following a 100 percent plant-based diet. In that moment I decided that I had nothing to lose. I had hit rock bottom, so eating plants rather than animals seemed like a better solution than amputation, no matter how crazy it might sound.

After a mere three weeks following a plant-based diet, I was off insulin completely!

It turns out that recognizing the dangers of the fats in animal products is one of the main keys to unlocking Type 2 diabetes, and it doesn't take much time of eschewing animal products for the body to reverse the damage. Additionally, animal products cause unnecessary stress on the body, which contributes even more damage to individuals already struggling with health problems like diabetes.

There are mounds of evidence about the health benefits derived from a plant-based diet. Doctors like Dr. Neal Barnard, Dr. Caldwell Esselstyn, Dr. T. Colin Campbell, Dr. Pam Popper, and Dr. McDougall are just a few who have poured years of research into the impact of what we eat and the diseases that we get. Meanwhile, the United States is becoming more and more a sick nation. Today, completely medicine-free, I know there is hope. I had been on medication for high cholesterol, high blood pressure, diabetes, hormonal problems, and for weight loss. I now have controlled blood sugar, my cholesterol went from near 400 to around 160, and I'm 150 pounds lighter. I do not have infections in my legs, and the nerve damage that was showing up in my legs and eyes is completely gone. The arthritis caused by the nerve damage is also gone.

In the end, the answer was easy, though finding it was challenging. Many medical doctors have not studied nutrition, nor do they read up on the many studies conducted regarding the preventive and healing benefits of plant-based nutrition. As my numbers changed, I explained to my doctor that I was on a plant-based diet. He replied that it "made sense," and that it was known that a plant-based diet can reverse Type 2 diabetes, but that it is "not convenient for most people." It was then that I realized I was no longer in need of his services.

Veganism is so simple in its conception, and it seems criminal that so few people have been told to try a vegan diet for healing and preventive health measures. Going vegan means showing compassion on many levels. For me, *compassion started with myself—treating my own body with respect and the care that it deserved.*

There are books out there that promise you massive weight loss, perfect skin, and boundless energy after going vegan, and while that may be the case for some, especially with the vast difference between the standard American diet and the vegan focus on whole foods, veganism is neither a miracle nor a cure-all. It's true, I have never felt better in my life, and I do have a greater energy level, but personally, I didn't shed pounds and suddenly become a supermodel. Hell, once you settle in and discover the wide world of vegan food, especially the sweets, you may find you haven't lost an ounce and may even be letting your belt out.

If you want to lose weight, there are great resources on how to do so with a vegan diet; check out *Appetite for Reduction* by Isa Chandra Moskowitz or *The McDougall Program* by Dr. John McDougall. Regardless, it takes more than diet for optimal health, so get ready for some exercise!

While it's a misconception that you have to be a health-food nut to be vegan, a diet full of processed vegan junk food is not only bad for you, but also bad for veganism, especially if your health suffers. Like everything in life, balance and moderation are key. Feel free to have an Oreo cookie (yes, they're vegan!) from time to time, if you desire it, but don't forget to eat your kale and quinoa!

GOING VEGAN FOR ENVIRONMENTALISM

Real environmentalists don't eat meat; this sentiment is expressed time and time again, offending Al Gore, Prius drivers, and reusable bag carriers everywhere. The reality is that the number-one thing you can do to reduce your carbon footprint is to go vegan! Wasted land, food, water, and energy, deforestation and biodiversity loss, water and air pollution—these are just a few of the environmental issues associated with factory farming and the meat industry.

Let's start with waste; according to *The Food Revolution* by John Robbins, it takes 5,000 gallons of water to produce 1 pound of meat, while growing 1 pound of wheat only requires 25 gallons. Nearly half of all the water used in the United States goes to raising animals for food! Need a visual? The beef in a hamburger could have been enough wheat to produce five loaves of bread. Currently about 2.6 billion people lack access to drinking water, and one thousand children die every day from dehydration. You actually save more water by not eating a pound of beef than you do by not showering for an entire year.

Scientists at the Smithsonian Institute have stated that the equivalent of seven football fields of land is bulldozed every *minute*, and much of it is to create more room for farmed animals. Of all the agricultural land in the United States, nearly 80 percent is used in some way to raise animals—about half of the United States' total land mass—and more than 260 million acres of U.S. forestland have been cleared to create cropland to grow grain to feed farmed animals! It's not only U.S. soil that's being used for animal agriculture; rain forests and ancient pine forests are also targeted, destroying ecosystems in order to fuel people's taste for flesh.

Speaking of destroying ecosystems, entire oceanic ecosystems are on the brink of collapse from the commercial fishing industry, which indiscriminately pulls as many fish as it can out of the sea. These reckless methods cause ecological devastation, push marine species to the brink of extinction, and kill other animals that are not being targeted, wasting countless lives.

According to Greenpeace, during the 2004–05 crop season, more than 2.9 million acres of rain forest were destroyed, and all of the native wild animals and trees were killed to grow crops that are used to feed animals in factory farms. Soy is a common crop grown in the rain forest, but not the soy we humans eat, which is primarily grown domestically. The rain-forest soy is used to feed farmed animals around the world, and 80 percent of the soy crops grown in the world are for animal feed. You have to wonder why these areas are being used to feed animals that are being eaten, when the land could be used to grow food for humans to consume themselves. Sadly, with the overgrazing comes the extinction of indigenous plants and animals, as well as soil erosion and desertification, irreparably damaging the land. At this time there may not be enough land left to grow crops for our growing world population.

Another result of animal agriculture is greenhouse gases, which contribute to global warming. Studies show that global warming will lead to worldwide disasters, such as droughts, floods, rising sea levels, hurricanes, and even disease outbreaks. The world's leading emitters of carbon dioxide (CO_2) are the factory farms that raise animals not only for their flesh, but also for the egg and dairy industries. CO_2 alone is not causing global warming; add methane and nitrous oxide emissions, and you have the source of the majority of global warming.

Let's talk about poop. Yes, really. The Worldwatch Institute says animals raised for food produce 130 times as much excrement as the entire U.S. population, roughly 89,000 pounds per second, all without the benefit of waste treatment systems. A pig farm with five thousand animals produces as much fecal waste as a city of fifty thousand people, according to the Waterkeeper Alliance and the Neuse Riverkeeper Foundation. Now *that* is a lot of poop, and it's affecting the health of humans, causing brain damage, depression, miscarriage and birth defects, bacterial infections, antibiotic resistance, and respiratory problems.

THE UNITED NATIONS REPORT ON GLOBAL WARMING AND LIVESTOCK

In 2006, a UN report called "Livestock's Long Shadow: Environmental Issues and Options" summarized the devastation caused by animal agriculture by calling it "one of the top two or three most significant contributors to the most serious environmental problems, at every scale from local to global." The report found that the livestock sector produces more greenhouse gases than all the SUVs, cars, trucks, planes, and ships in the world, *combined*.

Sections of the report included livestock in geographic transition as well as livestock's role in climate change, air and water pollution, water depletion, and loss of biodiversity. The most recent data available was used to make the assessment, and it took into account not only the direct impacts, but also the feed-crop agriculture required to sustain animal agriculture. Based on this report, senior UN Food and Agriculture Organization official Dr. Henning Steinfeld stated, "[U]rgent action is required to remedy the situation."

In 2010, the UN issued a new report, and the International Panel of Sustainable Resource Management stated, "A substantial reduction of impacts would only be possible with a substantial worldwide diet change."

Recently, the Worldwatch Institute issued a report claiming that the original 18 percent of annual worldwide greenhouse gas emissions attributed to livestock should be amended, as livestock accounts for at least 32.6 billion tons of carbon dioxide per year, or 51 percent of annual worldwide greenhouse emissions! Regardless of which report you look at, our environment is in dire straits, and there is no better way to take action than to remove yourself from the damage caused by livestock production and go vegan!

Teenuja
(Lovliebutterfly or Lovlie)

Location: I move around; I'm currently in Dublin, Ireland, but originally from Mauritius.

Blog: Vegan Lovlie (www.veganlovlie.com)

Reason You Went Vegan: It was a gradual process that started with the outbreak of mad cow disease in 2005, when I was in the UK. I stopped consuming all beef products at that time. After that came the avian flu, which made me stop eating chicken. I was a pescetarian for a while, and then I learned about animal cruelty. I watched a few videos on the subject, and that just did it! I became vegan in April 2007.

Favorite Dish to Cook: What else? Rich, decadent, chocolate cake with fudgy chocolate icing.

Funniest Vegan Moment: My most recent funny vegan moment actually happened at a wedding. In the evening, there was vegan food made especially for us (my boyfriend and me, plus some other vegetarians). However, at the buffet table, they did not label the vegan burgers, and as they looked more attractive (and were more tasty, as we learned later from the omnis who "stole" the burgers!), everyone grabbed them faster than I could. I was left without one. Luckily, the chef agreed to bring out some more!

OTHER ISSUES VEGANS CARE ABOUT

Many people assume that vegans only care about animals, and you may find yourself being accused of wanting to kill off humans in order to save animals, among other asinine accusations. The reality is that while many vegans are choosing to be a voice for animals, many (if not most) also concern themselves with human rights, such as the treatment of farm workers, and the rampant child labor and slavery found in the clothing and chocolate industries, for example. Others may tackle sustainability issues and encourage people to buy locally, avoiding processed goods with ingredients shipped from all over the world, including PVC shoes and accessories.

Some people devote their time to combating oppression, whether it's by making fresh produce available to low-income neighborhoods, working to remove fast-food restaurants from impoverished areas, or fighting sexism and embracing feminism. There are also people who care about all of these issues and work to make changes, as well as people who didn't come to veganism through animal rights at all, but through the rights of humans.

You don't have to be a single-issue activist; it is possible to care about a vast array of things in this world that need changing, and to work hard to change them.

WHAT IF I HAVE FOOD ALLERGIES?

While it may seem like allergies to foods such as soy, nuts, and wheat would make it impossible for people to go vegan, this is not the case at all. You can find resources on the Internet for gluten-free, soy-free, nut-free, and other vegan foods for people with food restrictions. In my circle of friends, we have a gluten-free vegan, someone with a peanut allergy, and another who tries to avoid soy, and yet we always have bountiful potlucks with a wide range of foods that everyone can partake in. Many companies are taking into consideration the growing allergy market, which is especially rampant in children these days. Vegans may find that they benefit from this, as many of these allergen-free foods are also suitable for a vegan diet. Ultimately, it is possible to find a wide range of allergen-free vegan foods with just a little research and an open mind.

FEMINISM AND VEGANISM

Many people believe that veganism and feminism go hand in hand, as female nonhuman animals are arguably the most exploited of all. Take the female cows of the dairy industry: These cows are repeatedly raped by farmers using a "rape rack" (the industry term) to impregnate them against their will. Shortly after birth, their babies are ripped from them to become veal, while humans consume the milk meant for their calves. The cows cry for their babies while they are repeatedly milked, then impregnated again, only to go through the same trauma, over and over. After a few years the cows are considered spent, and are sent to a slaughterhouse to become hamburger.

In today's society, animals are seen as lower beings, and yet women are called chicks, foxes, bitches, dogs, kittens, and cows. This is hardly something a feminist can endorse. If you believe in rights for women, or other oppressed groups, animals should be included on your list. Carol J. Adams, vegan feminist author, explores the link between meat-eating and the oppression of women in her groundbreaking book, *The Sexual Politics of Meat: A Feminist-Vegetarian Critical Theory*. It is a must-read for all feminists and those exploring how society treats females.

WHY HONEY IS NOT VEGAN

There is no doubt that a bee is a living being, and while you may think, "But they don't kill the bees for their honey," the issue is exploitation. It is actually not entirely accurate to say that bees are not killed in the farming of honey. Bees have a complex nervous system that allows them to feel pain, so it doesn't make sense to dismiss them as a lesser creature. To believe that honey is produced by a man in his backyard with a few hives is inaccurate. It is a much larger operation, not unlike a factory farm. Beekeepers have queen bees shipped to them, a cruel act in itself; then, in order to keep the worker bees active, the queen bee will be killed and switched out approximately every two years, despite the fact that the queen's life span is typically much longer. Bees are controlled by a smoker that causes them to unnaturally gorge themselves on honey, which calms them down and keeps them from stinging the keepers. Additionally, many beekeepers cruelly kill off their hives before winter, bees can be stepped on or smashed when the hives are checked on, and alarmed bees may sting people who invade their homes, causing them to die.

Oh, and another thing: Honey is bee puke. No, really. Bees swallow nectar, then regurgitate it, adding enzymes with their spit, then chewing and swallowing it repeatedly. There's your honey. Mmm, delicious!

Other products bees are exploited for are beeswax, which is secreted to build hives; royal jelly, which is bee food fed to worker bees to turn them into queens; and bee pollen, which is collected from the sacs on the bees' legs. These items are commonly found in cosmetics or sold as supplements, with claims to boost human health and vitality—at the expense of the bees, of course.

Laura

Location: San Francisco, California

Web Sites: Vegansaurus.com; VegWeb.com

Item You Can't Live Without: My rescued pit bull Hazel, and my Vitamix; that thing is *magic!* You can actually make soup in that sucker: Just put all the ingredients in and leave it for five minutes. It actually *boils*. Insane. Also, it can destroy everything from an unpeeled orange to an iPhone. Do not mess with the Vitamix!

Favorite Vegan Hater Comeback: "You're really good-looking . . . Do you want to go out sometime?" That always freaks people out.

Funniest Vegan Moment: I requested a vegan meal on a flight, but when we were in the air they didn't have it marked down, so I ate crackers and fruit. I was pissed because I love to eat. When we landed, I called the airline and they informed me that whoever took my message had written it down as "pagan" with a question mark. Like, why is this crazy lady telling me this? Anyway, amazing!

These days you can find alternatives to honey, such as agave nectar and honey-flavored syrups, like Suzanne's Specialties' rice nectar and Ohgave! organic honey-flavored syrup.

VARIATIONS OF THE VEGAN LIFESTYLE

Raw Foodists

While not all raw foodists are vegan, in my experience, many tend to be, and you'll run across raw restaurants and raw vegans around the world. Raw foodists believe that eating a diet of at least 75 percent raw food is optimal for health and energy levels. They also feel that raw and living foods contain enzymes, which aid in digestion, while food cooked at over 116 degrees Fahrenheit does not.

So, what exactly is raw food? Raw foodists emphasize the importance of not just plain vegetables and fruit, but also organic, unprocessed foods, like nuts, seeds, sprouts, sea vegetables, and fresh produce. Everything from raw pasta to pizza, sushi, crackers, bread, and even pies and cakes can be made, typically with the use of dehydrators, high-speed blenders, mandolins, or even just a great knife.

Many non-raw vegans enjoy raw food, myself included, and I can vouch for the desserts especially, as many of them are incredible! In the San Francisco Bay area, Café Gratitude has multiple locations, a loyal following, and a serious hippie vibe. Their taco salad keeps my husband and me coming back for more, while their tiramisu will make a believer out of anyone.

For more information on raw foodism, check out *Becoming Raw: The Essential Guide to Raw Vegan Diets*, by dietician Brenda Davis, Vesanto Melina, and Rynn Berry, and *Ani's Raw Food Essentials*, by Ani Phyo.

Macrobiotics

Another diet that is not exclusively vegan, but largely so, with many followers also choosing to be vegan, is the macrobiotic diet. Macrobiotic eating promotes wellness through a carefully balanced diet that emphasizes primarily whole grains, as well as vegetables, beans, seaweed, fruit, and fermented soy products. The diet also avoids highly processed and refined foods such as sugar and white flours. Occasional fish is included in the macrobiotic diet, but no dairy or other animal products are consumed. The diet focuses on balanced eating and includes guidelines for eating seasonally, with a focus on local foods. Popular among the Japanese, with many of the most prominent advocates being of Japanese descent, it's not uncommon to find macrobiotic restaurants in Japan—a great dining-out option for vegans. You can find more information in *Macrobiotics for Life* by Simon Brown, and *The Hip Chick's Guide to Macrobiotics* by Jessica Porter.

VEGAN VERSUS VEGETARIAN

While a vegan consumes no animal products, vegetarians only refrain from meat, and often still indulge in dairy, eggs, and honey. You may find some people don't know the difference, and you'll end up with cheese ravioli as your dinner option, so don't be afraid to be specific. While veganism is not new, it is only now breaking into mainstream consciousness, and we have a ways to go yet before all of society understands what the word means.

So, why go vegan instead of just going vegetarian?

Would you eat veal? Likely not, and many meat eaters shun veal as well. Unfortunately, the dairy industry and the veal industry are one and the same. For a cow to produce milk, the female must be impregnated. The female calves become dairy cows, which are eventually killed for meat, while the male calves become veal. By consuming dairy products, you're supporting the caging and slaughter of baby cows and allowing the industry to continue its cruel ways.

"I could never give up cheese!" is a declaration vegans hear more times than we could ever count. In reality, you *could* give up cheese; you'd just prefer not to, and you may very well be addicted. Studies by the Wellcome Research Laboratories in Research Triangle Park, North Carolina, have shown that casein, a milk protein found in cheese, can have an opiate-like effect, which is chemically addictive. The Physicians Committee for Responsible Medicine says, "Cheese contains far more casein than other dairy products do. As milk is turned into cheese, most of its water, whey proteins, and lactose sugar are removed, leaving behind concentrated casein and fat. Cheese holds other drug-like compounds as well. It contains an amphetamine-like chemical called phenylethylamine, or PEA, which is also found in chocolate and sausage."

Most vegans find that once they haven't had cheese for a while, and the casein is out of their systems, they'll no longer crave it. I know that this was true in my case. Also, the world of nondairy cheese is growing by leaps and bounds, so you'll likely find something out there that works for you if you're seriously feeling the need for a slice of pizza or some enchiladas. Another issue with cheese is that many of the producers use rennet; although this can be made from a vegetable source, it's more often than not made with cheaper ingredients that come from the lining of a cow's stomach—meaning your cheese may not even be vegetarian!

Luciana

Location: Gaithersburg, Maryland

Blog: Luciana's Vegan Kitchen (www.lucianaskitchen.com)

Reason You Went Vegan: For the animals, the planet, and my conscience.

Favorite Dish to Cook: Spanakopita from *Vegan with a Vengeance,* followed by chocolate cupcakes; it wins them over every time!

Funniest Vegan Moment: The first time I tried to cook tofu, I just dumped it into a pan with some sauce and expected it to come out as good as it did at my favorite Chinese restaurant. It looked so mushy and gross that I wouldn't even try it. I've learned a lot about cooking tofu since then!

The Free-Range Egg Myth

While many companies claim to have cage-free or free-range eggs, chickens are not protected by animal-cruelty laws; therefore, they can be kept in inhumane conditions with little to no repercussions, while still claiming to be cruelty-free. The U.S. Food and Drug Administration does not require disclosure of production methods on egg cartons, meaning the label "cage-free" or "free-range" is not regulated. Additionally, "free-range" does not mean that hens are allowed to wander around in the grass. Windowless sheds with a narrow exit leading to another enclosure are considered "cage-free," despite the areas being too small to accommodate all of the birds typically crammed in them.

All egg-laying hens come from the same hatcheries where male chicks, who cannot lay eggs, are ground up alive or suffocated to become feed or fertilizer. Hens have their beaks mutilated so they cannot injure each other when they're crowded together. Social creatures with nurturing instincts, hens typically live ten or more years, but when a hen's egg-laying production declines at about one or two years old, they are slaughtered to make room for "fresh" birds. The "spent" hens are typically so mutilated that they can only be ground up into fertilizer or sent to a landfill.

TRANSITIONING TO VEGANISM

Whether going from omnivore to vegan or vegetarian to vegan, some people find the adjustment a bit difficult, while others can go vegan at the drop of a hat. The first thing to remember is that nobody's perfect; there is a learning curve involved in eliminating animal products from your life, and you may find out when you're halfway through a box of crackers that they contain whey. Don't beat yourself up, and don't give up! Do the best you can every day and simply move on.

Some people find it easier to start by being vegan at home, and as vegan as possible while dining out, until they get the hang of things. Others take it one meal at a time and just try to do their best. I also know plenty of people who saw a documentary on animal cruelty, such as *Earthlings*, and never picked up an animal product again.

I started by eliminating cheese and eating all vegan savory food, but I found myself having trouble baking vegan. As I baked a few non-vegan things, I realized that my ethics were more important than cupcakes, so I went completely vegan and rose to the challenge of a new style of baking. Now, I have a vegan bakery, so you can see how well that went! Ultimately, for many people, going vegan is an ethical issue;

if you want to do what is morally right, you will strive to do just that and eliminate cruelty from your diet as fast as possible. Mistakes happen, but no one benefits when you "cheat" and knowingly eat something not vegan. I've never tasted anything that was so good; I would ignore the ingredients and my ethics just to have a bite. There's always a vegan alternative!

ANIMAL ACTIVISM

There are many ways to get involved in promoting veganism and animal rights issues. From grassroots campaigns to online activism, you can be a voice for the voiceless and help to spread the word. The key to success is to find the way you can be most effective. Whether you're a people person or a wallflower, there's a way for everyone to support the causes they care about.

Protests and Demonstrations

Despite the images projected in the media, animal activists aren't all aggressive, mask-wearing, red-paint throwers. There are plenty of peaceful ways to let people know about issues that are important to you. All over the world, people rally together to hold signs and pass out literature about circus cruelty, vivisection, poor animal welfare standards at establishments, puppy mills, and tons of other issues that the public is misinformed about or turns a blind eye to. I've participated in circus cruelty demonstrations, and it's amazing how many people are hearing about this for the first time. As with anything, there will be opposition, but with the support of your fellow activists and a level head, it can be a very rewarding experience to change the hearts and minds of others.

A simple way to reach the public is by leafleting. Giving someone the option to read a brochure on his or her own terms is a great way to get the word out without being pushy. One organization that has had great success spreading its message via leafleting is Vegan Outreach. Vegan Outreach has passed out over 11 million booklets to date, and I have heard of many people who read a brochure or saw a documentary, and couldn't fathom eating animal products afterward. Check out the Vegan Outreach "Adopt a College" program, where they place people on campuses to pass out literature. If you spent one hour a week passing out leaflets, think of how many people you could reach.

Letter writing is also an effective way to let others know where you stand on these issues. Don't be afraid to grab a pen and a piece of paper to inform local politicians about your stance on animal cruelty; to ask companies to expand their vegan options; to thank decision-makers for supporting animal causes; and to write letters to imprisoned activists. Stay aware of current animal issues in your area and join e-mail lists for organizations like Farm Sanctuary to find out when letters are needed. There are always plenty of letters to be written, so consider organizing a letter-writing party, where like-minded people can get together, chat about the issues, snack on vegan grub, and let their voices be heard.

Sometimes getting the word out about veganism is as easy as a few clicks. With social networking portals like Facebook, Twitter, blogs, and more, you can easily pass on articles and write opinion pieces to share with the world. Additionally, many animal rights groups have mailing lists to keep you up-to-date on petitions that need to be signed and letters that need to be written to decision-makers. Utilize this important tool to be an effective advocate.

Of course, not everyone is on board with veganism, and the Internet is a place where arguments and inflammatory comments can be made by faceless online warriors. While it's easy to engage in flame wars, share the joy of veganism instead by either ignoring the naysayers or giving well-thought-out and respectful statements backed up with facts to state your case. In the end, you have the option to pick your battles and focus on the positive. It doesn't do anyone any good when self-righteousness, name-calling, or ill-informed statements turn people off from an important issue.

Not yet ready to storm the streets wielding signs and a bullhorn? There are other ways to help animals and reach out to your local community.

The Worldwide Vegan Bake Sale is held yearly to raise awareness about veganism and to help fund various organizations. Bake sales are a great way to rally the locals and help the charities of your choice, as well as show people how delicious vegan baked goods are! You don't need a special event like the WVBS to have a benefit bake sale, however; it's easy to organize one anytime! The key factors are a good location, plenty of bakers, and successful advertising.

Try to find a busy location to hold your sale; many people find local businesses are often willing to host the event. Find a group of volunteers to bake treats, and consider providing recipes for those who are less familiar with vegan baking (the classics like cookies and cupcakes tend to do well). Advertise on the Internet and locally with flyers to inform people about the sale. Don't be afraid to contact local newspapers and TV and radio stations, as many media outlets are willing to cover charity events. Once your tables are set with treats and the signs are posted, watch the funds roll in! Don't forget to put vegan literature on the tables, like "Why Vegan?" leaflets by Vegan Outreach, so you can inform people about why you've made the ethical choices you have.

Did I mention that bake sales are fun? They're a great way to make new friends, learn about recipes, and eat lots of tasty baked goods! Win-win-win!

AVOIDING ACTIVIST BURNOUT

When you first go vegan, you may find yourself wanting to take on the world. Out of nowhere a new wardrobe of message tees fills your closet, you keep "Why Vegan?" leaflets in your bag, and when there's a demonstration or new animal rights campaign, you're there! This is great—the vegan community needs bright-eyed and bushy-tailed folks to spread the word in a positive way—but many people find that after a while, they get burned out. It's difficult feeling like no one understands you, especially when some people react with hostility when you're just trying to do the right thing. No activist is effective when they're stretched thin and unable to focus on the task at hand. You are far better off pacing yourself and doing as much as you can sanely handle than going for it and burning out after a few months, unable to participate in any activism at all. There are a lot of causes we need to support; discover what you are passionate about and devote yourself to it, but be sure to leave time for other things so you don't become a single-issue activist.

ORGANIZATIONS FOR ANIMAL ADVOCACY

You're not fighting this battle alone! There are organizations all over the world crusading for animals, environmental causes, and health. Farm Sanctuary, Physicians Committee for Responsible Medicine, the Humane Society of the United States, Viva!, Compassion Over Killing, Mercy for Animals, Vegan Outreach, Sea Shepherd Conservation Society, and In Defense of Animals are some of the leading voices working toward a more compassionate world. These organizations are always in need of volunteers and donations, so check them out and see how you can make a difference!

Roberta

Location: Italy

Blog: Ladybastard (ladybastard-harajuku.blogspot.com)

Reason You Went Vegan: In 2005, I saw a video about animal abuse. After that moment, something clicked in my brain, and I felt so guilty about consuming animal products. I felt like I was a part of that abuse, and from that moment, I stopped eating meat completely. In the beginning I was vegetarian, but after two years I became vegan! That was the best thing I've done in my life, both for me and for animals.

Favorite Dish to Cook: I totally love to bake cupcakes, and I also love to cook pasta.

Favorite Vegan Hater Comeback: Every day I meet a vegan hater! In Italy, people really don't understand this lifestyle. Most of them say to me: "Don't think about animals; think about the poor children who die because they don't have food!" My response is always the same: "As a vegan, I *do* think about poor people who don't have food. If everyone in this world was vegan, there would be so much food for everyone. The meat industry consumes so many resources of this world; it's the reason for most of the world's pollution, and of course, millions of animals die every day just because of man's greediness." If everyone in this world was vegan, the world would be a better place.

Just about everyone in the United States and beyond has heard of People for the Ethical Treatment of Animals, widely known as PETA. From throwing paint at fur wearers to ladies in lettuce bikinis, PETA is not afraid to make headline news. It is a misconception that if you are vegan, you are a supporter of PETA. Many vegans feel that to stop the exploitation of animals, PETA is exploiting humans, mainly female, by dressing them in skimpy outfits to gain attention. Of course, that is not the only thing PETA does, and while many people agree with what PETA stands for and choose to support select campaigns they have launched, it does not mean they agree with all of their tactics. Sensationalism and sex sells, and PETA knows that; you will have to decide for yourself if that is the route you want to take to advocate for animals.

ASK A VEGAN

When you live a lifestyle that is not the societal norm, people are bound to have questions. Whether it's a genuine curiosity or someone just trying to pull your strings, expect to field a variety of inquiries. While some are downright silly, others may be things you've wondered about as well. Consider this your starting point for answering the questions that are likely to be headed your way.

"No meat or dairy? What the hell do you eat?!"

This question can stump even the most seasoned vegan when they're put on the spot about what they consume. It's best to lay out some basics of vegan food, like beans, grains, vegetables, and fruits, and then tell people you enjoy most of the dishes they do, just without the animal products. Be sure to let them know you're not suffering through a steady diet of tofu and sprouts, and that vegan food is delicious!

"Where do you get your protein?"

Oh boy, if I had a dollar for every time someone asked me this! People can't seem to fathom protein without animal products, and yet protein is in most food, and the average person gets too much of it. Rather than laughing at them, let them know you get plenty of protein from beans, wheat, quinoa, nuts and seeds, and soy products like tempeh. If they don't seem to believe you, don't be afraid to let them know that Olympic gold medalist Carl Lewis won his medals on a vegan diet. Sometimes you just have to give them an impressive example to get them thinking.

"Why do vegans always want things that taste like meat? Why not just eat meat?"

Look—most vegans aren't saying that meat tastes disgusting, and they have always hated it. The reality is that most of us haven't been vegan since birth, and we have enjoyed a chicken wing or two in our past. It's not harmful to make animal-free replicas of the dishes we enjoyed before going vegan. It's often the texture you're looking for, and it can be replicated without hurting any living creature.

"If you were stranded on a deserted island with a cow/pig/ chicken, would you eat it?"

Let me just start by saying, don't answer this one. It's not likely you're ever going to be in a dire situation where you're forced to eat meat, so don't let people try to catch you in a situation where you question your ethics. Besides, I would eat whatever that cow was eating to survive; they're herbivores, after all.

"I'm a carnivore! Aren't canine teeth meant for eating meat?"

*First of all, humans are omnivores! People love to say we're carnivores, but the reality is, we don't need animal protein to survive. Many societies have gone without meat for centuries with no ill effects; look at studies of Buddhist monks. In the book **The China Study**, T. Colin Campbell explains that historically speaking, we only recently began eating meat. Meat and dairy are not necessary for survival, and a healthier lifestyle can be achieved by avoiding them.*

"Meat and cheese taste good; don't you miss them?"

*Sure, to most people, meat and dairy products **do** taste good, but it's not about taste—it's about ethics. For me, nothing tastes good when a creature had to suffer or die for it. I don't want to be a part of that misery. I personally don't miss meat and cheese; I'm eating better than I ever have, and vegan food is delicious! As my friend Isa says, "Your taste buds will catch up to your ethics," and I agree.*

"Veganism is too expensive! How can you afford it?"

Sure, if you only eat frozen veggie burgers, processed food, and dine out all the time, veganism can be costly! A diet of grains, beans, fruits, vegetables, and proteins like tofu, tempeh, and seitan are certainly less expensive than those pink slabs of flesh wrapped in plastic that most people call food. Compare the price of a pound of dried beans to a pound of beef, and then tell me how veganism is expensive. While processed products like dairy substitutes aren't inexpensive, the cost is not much more than their dairy counterparts, and you'll be saving money in the long run by cutting out all that meat. If you look at the staples of diets around the world—beans, rice, and breads—they tend to be vegan.

"Can't you just eat free-range eggs or organic meat?"

A "free-range" chicken or an "organic" cow does not know they're labeled as such; they only know they're not able to live their lives as it was intended. Regardless, free-range does not mean they're wandering free—only that they have access to the outdoors, and there's no requirements as to the size of that outdoor space. Only hens lay eggs, so male chicks are still killed in a grinder or sent to become food, regardless of the "cage-free" or "free-range" operation.

As for organic meat, while they may have more room to roam, they are still slaughtered in the same way as factory-farmed animals, making it no more humane. Try asking them this: How can you humanely **slaughter** an animal?

"You can't eat bread, right? Yeast is a living thing."

Despite the strange ongoing rumor, yeast is vegan; it is not a sentient being, so it's suitable for vegans. Beer is also fine, so long as it doesn't contain isinglass (learn more at Barnivore.com). You may find yourself being asked about very basic things like peanut butter, french fries, and even some fruits and vegetables, as many people don't entirely understand what is and is not vegan.

"Wouldn't cows explode if we didn't milk them?"

Do women's breasts explode if they don't breastfeed? While I'm not claiming it's comfortable for cows to have udders full of milk, if they didn't have their calves taken away, there would be a place for that milk to go. The reason cows produce milk is because farmers repeatedly impregnate them, which continues the milk cycle. Stop the cycle, stop the issue.

"Why don't you care about people?"

Some people assume that because you care about animals, you can't care about anything else. Obviously we know this is not true; people multitask all the time! While it's hard not to get offended and defensive, take the high road and let them know you **do** care about humans, and you're not a single-issue activist. Someone has to be a voice for the voiceless, whether they are human or nonhuman animals.

"But you don't look like a vegan! Aren't vegans all skinny and sickly?"

Oh no, you didn't! Oh yes, they did. Some people lack tact and think it's okay to tell a person their weight or physique doesn't correspond to society's stereotypical view of vegans. We don't all eat the same things, and we don't have the same genetics, cultural backgrounds, or upbringing. How can people expect us all to look the same? As for being sickly—what a joke! While many vegans are leaner than those eating the standard American diet, there are also vegan bodybuilders, athletes, and people of all shapes, sizes, and stature eating a vegan diet, and they're far from sickly.

"OMG, you can't eat that? Being vegan must be hard!"

Well, actually, I can eat that; I just choose not to. Sometimes people can't fathom their life without certain items, causing them to react strongly to your choice not to partake in something. I was one of those people who said I could never live without cheese, and look where I am now. Explain to them that you used to feel the same way, but now you find veganism easy. While some people have a tougher time going vegan, most find that once they get the hang of it, it's not a difficult thing to do.

TELLING OTHERS ABOUT VEGANISM

Once you've gone vegan, you may find yourself wanting to share your newfound knowledge with others, in hopes that they will join you. When you want others to go vegan, it's easy to be aggressive as you present the facts, just as it's hard to stand by helplessly when they choose to do nothing. While it's difficult to understand why no one wants to listen to you and why people say, "I don't want to know!" you have to understand that not everyone is going to be willing to listen, and what worked for you may not be what inspires them to go vegan.

Now, I'm not saying you should give up hope. The best thing you can do is live by example: Take every opportunity (when appropriate) to turn a conversation about diet or animals toward veganism, utilizing it to the fullest, and feed your friends and family generously to show them how delicious vegan food is. As much as you may want to push them, the worst thing you can do is be judgmental. Let them know you're open to talking about veganism if they're curious, and then don't cram it down their throats. Offer them books or links to Web sites that you have found to be effective for yourself and others. Appeal to their conscience by showing them successful animal rescue videos for all types of animals.

Many people think vegans are smug and preachy, while all we really want to do is help. If we want to succeed in helping to end animal suffering, it is necessary for us to find that balance between being helpful and harmful.

Monique

Location: Coachella, California

Blog: Mosetta Stone (mobettavegan. blogspot.com)

Favorite Dish to Cook: Seitan piccata; not just any, though. The one from Veganomicon turns omnivores into believers.

Favorite "Accidentally Vegan" Treat: Spicy Sweet Chili Doritos. I don't know how I did PB&J before these came along.

Funniest Vegan Moment: Every time I visit my parents, my dad always asks, "You do eat fish, right?"

Jojo

Location: Brighton, England

Blog: Vegan in Brighton (veganinbrighton.blogspot.com)

Reason You Went Vegan: I originally went vegan for animal rights reasons, as it just seemed the logical next step after vegetarianism. I realized I couldn't justify eating egg and milk products once I knew about the cruelty involved in those industries, so I just had to go vegan.

Favorite Dish to Cook: My absolute favorite dish to cook is the *New Farm Cookbook*'s macaroni and cheese. Aside from the fact that it tastes awesome, it's also easy to throw together after work or band practice, and even my cheese-eating friends love it!

Item You Can't Live Without: It has to be Special Effects hair dye. I've had brightly colored hair for years, and it's awesome that it comes in amazing colors and is also vegan and not tested on animals.

A man can live and be healthy without killing animals for food; therefore, if he eats meat, he participates in taking animal life merely for the sake of his appetite. And to act so is immoral.
—Leo Tolstoy

CHAPTER 2

NUTRITION

Nutrition is a subject that should be important to all, yet despite all of the knowledge that's available today, much of the world happily chows down on fast food, not considering the effects on their bodies, on animals, and on the planet. Ironically, vegans are tirelessly questioned about the health of their chosen diet on a regular basis.

A vegan diet is not only ethical, but it's nutritionally sound as well. The American Dietetic Association has approved a well-planned vegan diet for all people in all stages of life, including pregnant women, children, and the elderly. As long as you're eating foods from all colors of the rainbow, you should be able to get all of the nutrients necessary for your health without needing to become a supplement-popping freak. Of course, there's nothing wrong with a great multivitamin, but I'm not an expert in nutrition, so don't take my word for it.

Gena Hamshaw is a holistically trained, certified clinical nutritionist. Her practice is geared toward helping people find optimal health through plant-based nutrition. She works with clients in New York and around the world to find simple, affordable, and lasting healthy lifestyle habits, free of dieting cycles and emotional imbalance. She writes about body image, green living, and a plant-based lifestyle on her popular blog, Choosing Raw (www.choosingraw.com). This is not a purely raw food blog, but one that promotes a simple, sustainable, and nourishing lifestyle. Rather than give you my personal experience with nutrition, Gena is here to guide you on the basics. Take it away, Gena!

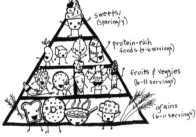

GREETINGS, VEGANISTAS!

Welcome to the wonderful world of vegan nutrition! It's time for you to learn all about fueling your body with plants.

I'm sure you have plenty of questions about eating a balanced vegan diet. This is normal! In this day and age, we're inundated with nutrition studies and information, and it's hard to separate fact from fiction. Fear not: I'm here to answer some of your most burning questions. Before I do, let me say this: It is 100 percent possible to eat not only a balanced diet, but also a downright *optimal* one, as a vegan woman. It may demand that you pay a little more attention to certain nutrients than your non-veganista friends do, but it's a tiny price to pay for living a cruelty-free, compassionate life. And once you master the basics of plant-based nutrition, you'll see that a vegan diet is among the world's most nutrient-rich and nourishing.

SO, WHERE DO YOU GET YOUR PROTEIN?

The first and most basic question that any new vegan should expect to be asked is this one. Most vegans find it irksome, if not plain old infuriating!

Before we analyze the basics of protein, let's analyze America's fixation with it. Here's the fundamental truth: Dairy, chicken, meat, and eggs offer us a great deal of protein. Unfortunately, they don't always offer us a great deal of other nutrients. True, all of these foods have some vitamin and mineral content, but the truth is that most of them can't compare to plant-based foods in terms of nutritional richness. Let's compare, for example, 4 ounces of steamed chicken breast with 1 cup of steamed kale. The chicken breast offers a great deal of protein (about 23 grams) and niacin. And that's about it. The kale, on the other hand, offers us hefty amounts of vitamins K, A, C, manganese, fiber, potassium, iron, folate, and magnesium, along with 10 percent of your daily calcium and a small serving of protein.

In other words, most plant-based foods—beans, vegetables, and whole grains, for example—are nutritional powerhouses. Animal proteins, on the other hand, are just that—they're proteins. They may offer a few other nutrients, but protein is the name of the game.

So, how do you sell a product that's protein-rich, but not necessarily a rock star  when it comes to other nutrients? Simple. By making the American public believe that it needs far more protein than it really does. Our protein mania (and fad diets like Atkins and South Beach) is no accident; it's the result of massive campaigning by meat and dairy companies to persuade us that protein is the single most vital nutrient around.

In reality, it is quite easy for an average man or woman to satisfy their protein needs. The World Health Organization estimates that a healthy man or woman ought to get approximately 10 to 15 percent of his or her calories from protein. For a person eating a 2,000-calorie diet, this is about 200 calories' worth of pure protein. To put it in more-direct terms, most health professionals agree that an average man needs approximately 56 grams of protein daily, and an average woman needs approximately 46 grams.

The good news is that these numbers are staggeringly easy to attain. Let's look at a balanced day of vegan food:

Breakfast

A bowl of oat bran with a tablespoon of almond butter and a banana (14 grams)

Snack

1 ounce raw almonds (6 grams)

Lunch

2 tablespoons hummus and ¼ sliced avocado on whole-grain bread with 1 cup of Basic Lentil Soup (recipe on page 148) and a salad of spinach and mixed vegetables (approximately 20 grams)

Snack

Vegan snack bar (approximately 7 grams)

Dinner

½ cup quinoa (cooked), one serving of Basic Three-Bean Chili (recipe on page 177), 1 cup steamed broccoli, and tahini dressing (approximately 20 grams)

That is *67 grams* of protein—well over the recommended daily requirement! The fact that it's so easy to obtain adequate protein within a vegan model really ought to be no surprise, as protein exists in virtually all foods, plant and animal alike. Unless one is failing to eat enough or to sustain body weight, then it's nearly impossible to become deficient in protein.

Proteins comprise a variety of amino acids. It was once thought that one had to eat various plant foods in combinations (such as rice and beans) within a single meal in order to get "complete proteins"—that is, proteins containing all the necessary amino acids. Recent research, however, suggests that it is in fact possible for the body to build its own complete proteins, just so long as one eats a variety of plant-based foods over the course of a given day.

Finally, it's worth pointing out that excessive protein has been directly linked to kidney disease, since high-protein diets flood our bodies with excess nitrogen, which the kidneys then struggle to filter out through urine. It has also been linked to some types of cancer, osteoporosis, and kidney stones.

WHAT ABOUT CALCIUM?

This question is slightly more apropos than the protein query, because unlike protein, which exists in nearly all foods, calcium can be a slightly more elusive nutrient. It is, however, absolutely vital for human health. It not only helps us to maintain our strong bones (its most famous function), but it also aids in blood clotting and is vital for our nervous system. With vigilance and care, it's not hard to get all you need within a vegan diet. The top vegan sources of calcium include:

- Certain dark leafy greens, like collards, turnip greens, kale, and broccoli
- Blackstrap molasses
- Tofu and tempeh
- Calcium-fortified soy, almond, oat, or hemp milk
- Tahini and sesame seeds
- Almonds and almond butter

This list doesn't include calcium-fortified orange juice and cereals, which are also abundant!

The average adult needs upwards of 1,000 mg of calcium daily; the average woman over the age of fifty (which is to say, women who are peri- or postmenopausal) might do well to get upwards of 1,200 mg daily. As you've probably heard, it's difficult for our bodies to absorb calcium without vitamin D, which is, in theory, naturally occurring in the human body, developing from our exposure to sunlight. Due to the fact that most of us work desk jobs, however, and wear sunblock during the short time we are outside, many adults are becoming prone to vitamin D deficiency. To allay this, it's very wise for all vegans to consider taking a vitamin D supplement, as the most-common food sources (egg yolks, saltwater fish, liver, and fortified milk) are not vegan-friendly. A dosage of 2,000 IU daily or less is sufficient for most adults; many calcium supplements are now fortified with vitamin D automatically.

So what would a calcium-rich day look like for a vegan? Easy!

Breakfast

1 cup calcium-fortified soy or oat milk (300 mg), one entree serving of Two-Bean Confetti Hash (recipe on page 139) (50 mg)

Lunch

Scrambled tofu (20 mg) with kale or collard greens (170 mg), toast

Dinner

Steamed broccoli and bok choy (250 mg), Brussels Sprouts with Crispy Tempeh over Soft Polenta (recipe on page 161) (140 mg)

Dessert

5 dried figs (56 mg)

A total of 986 mg—and easy as pie!

For those of you who are still fretting about protein, here's a little food for thought: Some studies have shown that high-protein diets can decrease calcium absorption, which means that our bodies will leach calcium from our bones as a response. All the more reason to abandon your porterhouse and whey protein and discover the joys of beans and greens!

IRON

Iron, like calcium, can be a little tricky to get a hold of. In addition to this, the kind of iron found in plant foods (non-heme iron) isn't quite as easily absorbed by the body as the heme iron found in animal foods. For this reason, vegans might want to increase their iron goals each day. Menstruating females should also be mindful that they need to get more iron than men; a good ballpark range is 10 to 15 mg daily for vegan men, and 15 to 20 mg daily for vegan women.

As for finding sources of iron, fear not: Like every other major nutrient group, iron is readily available within a vegan paradigm. Dark, leafy greens—including spinach, chard, kale, bok choy, beet, and turnip greens—are stellar sources! Some other major iron contributors include:

- Blackstrap molasses
- Lentils
- Soybeans

Leigh

Business Name: Cosmo's Vegan Shoppe
Web Site / Location: www.cosmosveganshoppe.com; Marietta, Georgia

Do you put an emphasis on the vegan aspect of the company, and, if so, do you find it works in your favor?

We are all about promoting veganism! Since "vegan" is in our business name, we get plenty of chances to answer questions about what vegan means, why we are vegan, animal rights, etc. Our whole business model is to provide specialty products to vegans, so I think it is working in our favor.

How do you handle any animosity toward veganism in your personal life or business?

Of course, some animosity comes up from time to time, and before we started Cosmo's, I'll admit I didn't always keep my cool when faced with combative people. Now with the business, I especially want to come across as a normal, intelligent woman who just happens to be vegan and an animal rights activist. So unless someone is just trying to push my buttons, I will do my best to kill 'em with kindness—and maybe some vegan baked goods!

What's your favorite item that you sell?

It's hard to choose just one! I'm a huge fan of vegan cookbooks, so I try to stock all the newest and best titles available. I also eat way too many awesome sweets thanks to the selection of Sjaak's Organic Chocolates and Liz Lovely Cookies we stock.

Favorite vegan meal (to cook or when dining out)?

I love breakfast food! Especially breakfasts of the savory variety. Tofu scramble, country-style biscuits and gravy, vegan omelets, and the occasional stack of pancakes suit me just fine. I love all kinds of vegan food, and think about what I'm going to cook or bake pretty much all the time. That can't be normal, can it?

- Quinoa
- Tofu and tempeh
- Black beans
- Kidney beans
- Black-eyed peas
- Dried apricots
- Raisins
- Tahini/sesame seeds

An iron-rich day of food for a vegan might include:

Breakfast

Tofu scramble with spinach and toast (approximately 6 mg)

Lunch

1 cup lightly steamed baby spinach (approximately 3 mg)
Roasted Balsamic Cauliflower and Cannellini Beans (recipe on page 154) (approximately 5 mg)

Snack

Raisins and almonds (approximately 2 mg)

Dinner

Moroccan Chickpea and Kale Tagine with Quinoa (recipe on page 168) (4.5 mg)
That's a total of 20.5 mg—well within the RDA for women.

If your blood work ever indicates low iron levels, you may want to try having a tablespoon of blackstrap molasses each morning (straight up, or in a bowl of hot cereal). It's a concentrated iron source and may give you the boost you need. If that's not effective, you can consider a vegan iron supplement.

Keep in mind, too, that our bodies absorb iron better when we're also eating vitamin C. So it's a great idea to throw some citrus fruit or fennel into your spinach salad!

VITAMIN B12

Clearly, it's not hard to get all the nutrients you need within a balanced vegan diet. There is one vitamin, however, that doesn't occur naturally in a vegan diet, and that's B12. We

Emiko Badillo

Business Name: Food Fight! Vegan Grocery

Web Site / Location: www.foodfightgrocery.com; 1217 S. E. Stark Street, Portland, Oregon

What motivated you to start your business?

My husband and I moved to Portland in 2002, it was a bit less vegan-crazy back then. We found ourselves having to shop at three different stores to get all the kinds of foods we wanted. We thought it'd be a good service to open a store that would have everything in one place, and where vegans could feel safe, not having to shop in a place that sold meat and dairy (even though they knew their money wasn't going to fund those departments). It's so gross to shop at those regular stores and have to walk past all the dead animals and the smell of the cheese.

You're reaching for your vegan cheese, and right next to it is a package of dairy cheese! At this one grocery store in Portland, the produce department is right next to the meat department. We also wanted to focus on breaking stereo-types of what veganism was (and is), to show that it's not the bland "hippie" food other people think it is. We wanted to make omnivores see that our food is more fun.

Do you put an emphasis on the vegan aspect of the company, and, if so, do you find it works in your favor?

Yes, very much. There was no question that we wanted the word "vegan" in our name; it jelled with our mission to break stereotypes. Boom. We're vegan. We're showing veganism isn't boring. We're a vegan store, and we're proud. Fuck it—why hide it? One person told us that the world "isn't ready" to see the word used so unapologetically, and he suggested using "veg" instead. He made us all the more sure that we wanted to use "vegan," and also that we wanted to put our politics and personalities into our store as much as possible. We're still around after all these years. I'm sure plenty of people who come in don't like our take on veganism, but, oh well.

What's the most rewarding part of running a vegan business?

When people come in, and say "This _____ made me finally go all the way vegan!" Or when I hear about more and more vegan businesses opening up all the time; plus, all our awesome regular customers who come in to buy all their food for the week from us. We like when people use the store like a full-fledged grocery rather than a novelty store—but we love all our customers.

What's your favorite item that you sell?

Earthlings (the documentary).

don't need much B12, but we can only get the small amount we do need from animal products, so vegans need to seek out a supplement. It's true that there is some B12 in fermented-soy products, fortified nutritional yeast, and seaweed, but these aren't reliable sources, and the B12 we find in them is pretty scant. Therefore, it's best for all vegans to rely on B12-fortified foods (such as soy milk or breakfast cereals), or to take a high-quality vegan supplement, available in a full-spectrum B vitamin, in a multivitamin that caters to vegans (such as the Garden of Life Vitamin Code line), or on its own.

OMEGA-3s

Omega-3 fatty acids have only hit the nutrition headlines recently, but now that they have, we're all paying attention. They're an important part of the human diet, and they play a role in combating conditions from allergies and arthritis to diabetes, eczema, stroke, and weight gain. We all know by now (or if you don't, I'll tell you) that there are various types of fatty acids. It's the saturated fatty acids that contribute to cholesterol and heart disease, among other things, and these are the ones we need to watch out for. Monounsaturated and polyunsaturated fatty acids, on the other hand, can help to lower LDL ("bad") cholesterol.

Then there are the essential fatty acids, omega-6s and omega-3s, which are called essential because we need to ingest them directly. In other words, unlike complete proteins, we can't just assemble them from various food sources. These help to fight inflammation and stabilize your mood, among other things. While most Americans get a good number of omega-6 fatty acids in their diets, most of us don't get enough omega-3s. (An ideal dietary ratio of omega-3s to omega-6s would be 1:4; many Americans have a ratio of 1:20 instead.)

The most commonly known plant-based omega-3 is alpha-linolenic acid (or ALA). When it's broken down in the human body (with the aid of certain vitamins), ALA can be converted into two other acids: EPA (eicosapentaenoic acid) and DHA (docosahexaenoic acid). It isn't always easy for the body to convert ALA to EPA and DHA. To get DHA directly—without the body's conversion—one would have to rely on a fish source (salmon oil and other fish oils are the most common) or an algae source, usually found in supplemental form. For vegans, this leaves a few options:

- Take an algae-based vegan DHA supplement.
- Be sure to put blue-green algae in a morning smoothie.
- Check out a vegan, DHA-rich oil blend.

The latter are increasingly available on the market. Lately, I've been enjoying the Vega EFA oil blend for a spectrum of fatty acids. For DHA specifically, Udo's Oils makes an oil blend that is very high quality. Any one of these options should help you to meet your omega-3 needs in a jiffy!

IS SOY SAFE?

For decades, soy foods have been presented as the mainstay of a vegan diet. The word *tofu* is synonymous with *health food* in the popular imagination, and soy lattes are immediately associated with the health- and body-conscious. There's good reason for this: Soy foods—particularly tofu and tempeh—are rich in calcium and protein. They are also low in fat, and they've been associated with the reduction of LDL ("bad" cholesterol) in certain studies. Soy foods also contain plant-based estrogens (phytoestrogens) that have been proven to help some women avoid the more unpleasant side effects of menopause.

Recently, however, there's been more critical scrutiny of soy foods. Many whole foods advocates note that soy foods are usually processed to some degree. Others point out that the estrogens in soy are, if not hazardous in and of themselves, unsettling for certain women, especially those who are concerned about breast cancer. Finally, soy foods are goitrogens, which means that they're not safe for people with thyroid conditions.

Who to believe? Remember that when we discuss soy's potential harm, we're essentially discussing what soy can or can't do when eaten *very habitually or even excessively*. Many doctors and experts point out that Asian populations have been eating soy for ages without the apparent health problems that some of us are now attributing to it. This is true, mostly because those same Asian populations eat soy moderately and in less-processed forms than we do. We might like to think of soy as a health fanatic's dream food, but it's actually hidden in a number of unhealthy foods: Soy by-products make an appearance in nearly all processed foods. So while Asian populations may love tofu, they also don't tend to eat soy habitually in the form of snack bars, packaged snacks, and even breads.

The bottom line? Eat soy in moderation, and in as unprocessed a form as possible. Edamame is obviously the least processed. Tempeh, which is fermented, is also a great option. And when you purchase tofu, opt for organic and non-GMO (genetically modified organism), if at all possible, since soybeans are a major GMO crop. Also check your farmers' market for handmade tofu; more and more markets are starting to carry artisanal tofus, which bear a close resemblance to the tofu made in East Asia.

If you're having a really lousy day, relax and have that soy milkshake. Occasional processed soy treats certainly won't do you any harm—not when eaten sensibly and with balance in mind.

THE UPSHOT

Getting what you need as a vegan is far less complicated than some dieticians would have you believe. With a little diligence—and a lot of dark, leafy greens—you'll be well on your way to feeling your most vibrant and healthy. Enjoy the journey!

—Gena Hamshaw, clinical nutritionist

VEGANISM AND PREGNANCY

It's easy to doubt yourself when you get pregnant and everyone around you asks, "You're not going to stay vegan, are you?!" The reality is, a vegan diet is perfectly healthy for all phases of life, including pregnancy. All pregnancies should be well planned to make sure your baby is getting the proper nutrition. Work with a supportive doctor and do your research to ensure a healthy pregnancy. The biggest challenge may be sticking to your ethics when you have cravings for non-vegan items. Vegan women I have spoken to have admitted to cravings, but most are able to push through and eat something vegan, and those who admitted to giving in to cravings expressed remorse. The bottom line is, you have to do what is best for you and your child, and veganism is not a determent to good health as long as you are educated.

RAISING VEGAN CHILDREN

Feeding children a vegan diet is not only healthy and compassionate, but it can also be easy as well. Children tend to enjoy the foods they're exposed to, so you can set your children off on the right foot by feeding them a plant-based diet. Many kid-friendly foods are vegan or easily can be, such as peanut butter and jelly sandwiches, spaghetti with tomato sauce, soup, baked potatoes, pancakes, waffles, rice and beans, and tacos. I know plenty of parents whose kids drink green smoothies, love kale, and don't bat a lash at quinoa. Sometimes you may find that presenting things in a creative way will work in your favor, whether it's using a large cookie cutter for shaped sandwiches, or layering apple slices to look like an animal with pretzel feet! When snack time comes around, look to simple menu items to keep your kids happy, such as the celery, peanut butter, and raisin combo ("ants on a log"); hummus and tortilla roll-ups with vegetables; assorted fruit on skewers; bagels with a spread; vegetable sticks with dip; pretzels with peanut butter for dipping; dried fruit; or popcorn sprinkled with nutritional yeast. Other resources that provide helpful food ideas for kids are the Vegan Dad blog, and the book *Vegan Lunch Box*, by Jennifer McCann.

If your child is older when you transition to veganism, you may have a more-difficult time if they're already set in their ways when it comes to what they like to eat. In most cases, you can find a vegan counterpart to their favorites, such as chicken-less nuggets, pizza with soy cheese, nondairy mac and cheese, and even meatless deli slices for sandwiches. Ideally, they won't be living off these processed foods, but they're a great way to transition to veganism as you start to incorporate new food items into their diet.

VEGAN ATHLETES

There's a misconception that athletes have dietary needs that keep them from being vegan. The reality is, runner Carl Lewis was at his peak performance and won his Olympic gold medals on a vegan diet. Endurance runner and vegan Scott Jurek recently ran more than 165.7 miles in twenty-four hours, setting an American record. Dr. Ruth Heidrich is a six-time Ironman Triathlon finisher, holder of more than nine hundred gold medals, and a vegan for more than twenty-five years. With groups like Organic Athletes and Vegan Bodybuilding, it's easier than ever to get the proper tools to get fit using plant power, and prove that you're not only strong, but eating an optimal diet for peak performance!

Christine Vardaros, a world-class cyclocross racer, is a prime example of how a vegan diet and athleticism can go hand in hand (see page 56).

Laviyah

Location: Chicago, Illinois

Web Site: Ste Martaen Vegan Cheese (www.stemartaen.com)

Kids' Names and Ages: Zerahkyah (age eleven), Tesher (age nine), Yaphet (age three), and Elianna (age one)

Why did you go vegan?

Spiritual and ethical reasons; it's unnecessary to hurt, maim, and murder animals in order to eat. What type of karma am I emitting by supporting death?

What advice do you have for people who want to raise their children vegan?

It is possible to raise healthy children on a vegan diet. Make sure to include a large variety of foods. Breastfeed! My children will eat most fruits, grains, legumes, and vegetables. I make sesame-seed milk every other day. A typical week may be brown rice waffles, veggie burgers, chickpeas and rice, scrambled tofu, homemade bread, quinoa, kale salad, fruit salad, and our Ste Martaen cheese, of course. I make the waffles from scratch. I also buy dried beans, soak them, and cook them in the Crock-Pot. My husband makes veggie burgers from scratch. The children get a very good example of the process of cooking, how to create a meal, and that being vegan is delicious; it's really all they know. And we never, ever use a microwave.

How do you deal with the naysayers?

I don't. People have their opinions. My happy, healthy children are enough for me. I don't get into arguments with people. I do what I believe is best for my children, period.

What are your kids' favorite foods?

Zerahkyah loves tomatoes, Tesher loves oatmeal, Yaphet loves hummus, Elianna loves strawberries.

What are some quick and easy snacks you always have on hand?

We love Trader Joe's. They're a great resource for inexpensive vegan snack foods. We get peanut butter pretzels from them, unsweetened applesauce, raisins, and dehydrated strawberries. They also make vegan rice crispy treats, a rare snack; I try to keep snack-time sugar-free. I also buy pineapple cups and a bag or two of low-salt roasted peanuts, and organic blue corn chips for homemade nachos.

Do you find you have to push certain healthy foods on them, and do you supplement their daily intake with vitamins?

The children do take vitamins, mainly because I read up on the mineral and vitamin content of foods grown in America, and found that the vitamin and nutrient content is lacking. An orange from 1921 had more vitamin C than an orange of today. The crops here in the United States are grown in soil that is seriously depleted of nutrient and mineral content. You will not find anything with high fructose corn syrup in my house; I make it a point to avoid foods with added sugars and artificial sweeteners.

My child has decided to go vegan; now what?

Many parents are faced with their child making the compassionate choice to go vegan at a young age. I went vegetarian at thirteen, despite growing up in a "steak and potatoes" household, and my family was baffled. As a parent, the best thing you can do is to be supportive, even if you're not happy about their choice. Don't treat your child as if it's "just a phase." Respect that they're making a decision about how they want to live, and don't be afraid to discuss with them why they've made this choice. Growing children have nutritional needs that can easily be addressed by a vegan diet, but some research is required. I recommend that parents read up on dietary needs and then talk to their children about nutrition. Ask them to do some research themselves. If children want to make a life-changing decision, they should share the responsibility to keep themselves healthy. The Vegetarian Resource Group is an excellent online resource that includes a section on raising children on a plant-based diet.

Christine "Peanut" Vardaros

Location: Everberg, Belgium, by way of New York City and Mill Valley, California
Sport/Teams: Current team: Zannata-Champion System Pro Cycling Team
Christine turned pro in 1999, and for the last ten years, she represented the United States at World Cup and World Championship races.

What was the reason you went vegan?

I originally went vegetarian on a whim. Twenty years ago, my best friend asked me, "Wanna go vegetarian? If everyone were vegetarian, we could feed the world four times over!" My immediate response was, "That sounds great—but what is a vegetarian?" From that moment forward, we were vegetarians.

Ten years later, I went vegan. I cut out the dairy when I became a pro cyclist in 1999, since it was getting in the way of breathing. Shortly afterwards I became completely vegan—partly for health reasons—but I can guarantee you, I will never go back to eating a single piece of flesh or partaking in anything that has any speck of an animal in it, due to the moral reasons. I am a spokesperson for IDA (In Defense of

Animals), as well as Organic Athlete, and I give talks around the world on the athletic performance benefits of a plant-based diet.

What are the misconceptions about veganism in the cycling world? How do you handle the naysayers?

People think you can't get enough calories or even enough protein on a vegan diet, which is completely false. Normally I let my results speak for themselves, but I also address this in the talks I give. Basically, you'd have to be starving and in a Third World country to not get enough protein. In fact, during heaving training periods, I try to cut my protein intake down even more for recovery purposes, since protein is so detrimental to the body—especially an athletic one.

Do you find it difficult to eat a balanced, calorie-rich vegan diet while training?

It is easy to get all my calories—up to 5,000 a day, in fact—on a vegan diet. I can eat 90 percent of what you find in your average super-market.

What keeps you motivated to push yourself?

I ride for the animals and to serve as an example that a vegan diet is not only possible, but also ideal for top-level sports. I've learned so much about myself through cycling.

VEGANISM AND EATING DISORDERS

You may wonder why eating disorders would be mentioned in a book about veganism, but unfortunately, there has been some connection between the two. People with eating disorders, especially anorexia, have been known to claim to be vegetarian or vegan to prevent themselves from having to eat in front of others. People may try to use this as an argument against a vegan diet, which can be very frustrating when you do not actually have disordered eating. Veganism should be an opportunity to seek out variety in your diet, and is not a means of restriction.

When a disordered mind-set is present and someone goes vegan, they may find themselves going overboard on restrictions, whether it be soy-free, gluten-free, fat-free, or other rules they inflict on themselves. This is not to say there are not people who genuinely have medical conditions where they need to have a mindful diet, but many times people are choosing not to partake in the diverse world of vegan food due to other issues. Food blogs can occasionally trigger people with eating disorders; other factors include a lack of nutritional meals and dietary diversity, and obsessive talk of calories, exercise, and health—detrimental for anyone with disordered eating tendencies.

Veganism and eating disorders are not mutually exclusive. Most eating disorders have little to do with the actual food being consumed, but actually stem from other underlying issues. You can care about animals and/or the environment and still have an issue with disordered eating, which can be treated while sticking to your ethics. If

Silvia

Location: Ferrara, Italy

Website: www.flickr.com/photos/milvialovesyou

Reason You Went Vegan: I went vegetarian when I was fifteen years old, and after some years, I went vegan. I'm vegan because I'm against animal and environmental exploitation. For that reason, I choose to be not only vegetarian, but vegan. Dairy products are like meat—products of battery farming. In any case, I can't eat something living, and the vegan diet is healthy and "positive" because it does not include dead animals. I don't know; I think that choosing to be vegan is not a simple dietary choice, but a choice of lifestyle.

Item You Can't Live Without: Music; I bake and cook, live and love, listening to music.

Funniest Vegan Moment: My boyfriend and I were drinking at our friends' bar. For the aperitif there was bread, white rice, tomatoes, chips, green and black olives, sweet onions, carrots, and slices of grilled polenta. We asked if it was all okay for us to eat, and they replied, "Yes, of course!" So, we bit into a slice of polenta, and *blechh!* What a strange taste! "Yes, on the polenta there is a thin slice of lard." *What—lard?* "Yes, but it's very thin. Thin, thin, I assure you."

you came to veganism through an eating disorder, not all has to be lost. I know a fair amount of people who have used veganism as a tool in their recovery, developing a healthy relationship with food by being involved with the enjoyment many people find in documenting meals they enjoy. Here is a recovery story from my good friend, Gabrielle. I am so proud of what she has accomplished and the happy and healthy person she is today:

I suffered for years with anorexia, and sparing you all the tales of sickness and rock-bottoms, I'd much rather recount how I recovered.

Eating disorders are, in most cases, symptoms of greater distress. Therefore, when one enters treatment due to the visible symptoms, it is far more beneficial for the treatment providers to zero in on the root cause rather than to immediately and forcefully change a person's eating habits.

However, this isn't entirely possible for those in the throes of the illness, with severely compromised bodies. Once medical stability is achieved (and ideally, treatment will soon be more readily available before this point is reached), it is most effective for the treatment providers to focus on unearthing whatever issue is making a sufferer feel undeserving of a healthy life. I was lucky enough to work with people who operated in this vein, and so, following my medical stabilization, we then focused on those issues that were causing my self-compromising behavior.

In learning to give my body the nutritious food that it deserved, I had a lot of hesitation about just what I wanted to put in my body. I'd been vegetarian for years before this point in my recovery, but I was often challenged into thinking that perhaps this choice had more to do with restrictions than ethics. However, while I learned to trust my own feelings and instincts, I recognized that one of the reasons I had such a tenuous relationship with food is that ethically, I simply didn't want to be eating animal products. It wasn't a matter of choosing a low-calorie plate of salad over eggs Benedict. I eventually got to the point where I'd grab a vegan cupcake, and feel much better about eating it than consuming a low-fat egg-white omelet. I knew that, for a multitude of reasons, veganism was right for me.

Even today, as a happy and healthy normal-weight person, I'm often tentatively questioned by well-meaning people who assume that my dietary choices are still symptoms of a past eating disorder. Let me tell you, they

Melanie

Location: Vienna, Austria

Blog: Vegan Foodism (www.veganfoodism.com)

Reason You Went Vegan: I went vegetarian for the animals, and then vegan on a dare. Two vegans I used to hang out with told me I was too lazy and would go back to my vegetarian ways after a few weeks. That was almost fifteen years ago, and I have never looked back. Best decision I ever made for the animals, my health, and the environment.

Favorite Dish to Cook: I love veganizing Austrian home cooking, and I make a mean lentil stew with dumplings that no one can resist.

Favorite Vegan Hater Comeback: "I can't eat meat because I am allergic to animal cruelty!"

are not! I have never felt so appreciative of my food, so excited about the welcome challenge of veganizing everything, so happy that I am not supporting an industry that causes animals to suffer in order to feed human beings substances that they don't even need, and that are more often than not detrimental to our health.

I can easily say that veganism played a large role in the latter stages of my recovery. The key is to focus on why you are vegan, rather than getting sucked into the eating-disordered mind-set that craves restriction. Some people will tell you that you will never fully recover from an eating disorder, but that is not true. I am fully recovered, and yes, after many frightening hospital stays, some suicide attempts, and the general prognosis (as communicated to myself and my family as bleak and hopeless), one step at a time, I pulled through. And I have never been happier.

With a bit of diligence, you'll be on your way to eating a nutritionally balanced diet without harming other beings. The standard American diet is nutritionally devoid, so know that you're already taking a fabulous step toward good health by avoiding cholesterol-laden foods. While a whole foods diet is optimal, the key is to have fun with your food, eat a diverse range of foods, and most of all, to *enjoy* what you're eating. Moderation and balance will ensure that you live a long and happy life, while treading lightly on the Earth!

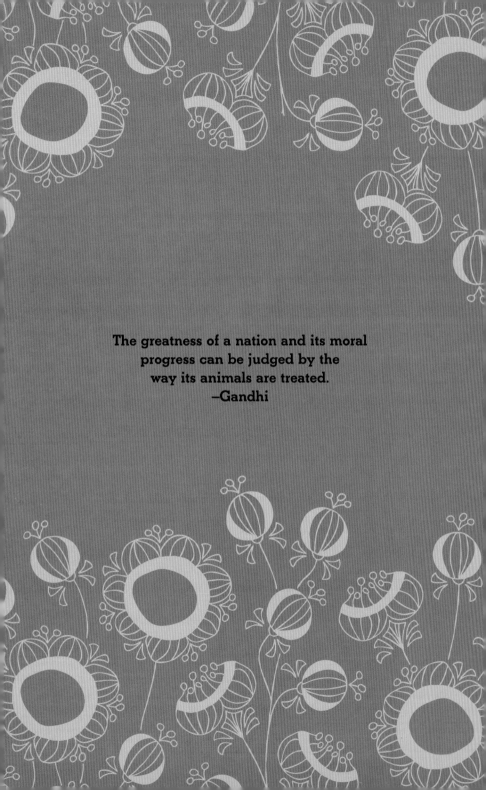

The greatness of a nation and its moral
progress can be judged by the
way its animals are treated.
—Gandhi

CHAPTER 3

VEGAN LIVING

So, you've gone vegan. Your friends think you're crazy because you read the ingredients of everything, ask waiters a million questions, and can't help but check the Barnivore iPhone app before each sip of alcohol you take. Don't worry—the social awkwardness will subside, and you can take comfort in knowing you're doing what's best for the animals, the environment, and for your own health. In the meantime, there are ways to make the transition comfortable for everyone.

Some people find that being surrounded by people who don't understand their lifestyle choice is very frustrating. Whether they are simply uninformed about the plight of animals, or they haven't yet come to the conclusions you have about veganism, it is important for you to lead by example. Nonetheless, it's tough when you're trying to do something good and no one else seems to get it, or to care. Your frustration may be increased because jokes are constantly made at your expense, or because you are often the target of verbal attacks from "well-meaning" family members, or because you find yourself stuck at a table covered with a selection of animal flesh and butter-laden vegetable dishes.

The last thing you want to do is seem like a whiny pain in the ass when you're not with people who are vegan. Veganism really doesn't have to be difficult, and acting as though it is a constant struggle may turn people away from learning more about it. While being vegan in a non-vegan world can feel challenging, arming yourself with options, answers, and coping mechanisms can lead to calmer waters, and you may even gain some new recruits and new friends along the way.

Many vegans turn to the Internet to find like-minded people they can have discussions with, and of whom they can ask advice when things get rough. It's nice to have both a sense of camaraderie with others and also a sometimes-mindless escape from the day-to-day routine; message boards can provide that. Some popular sites for vegan discussion are VegWeb.com, the Post Punk Kitchen (www.theppk.com, my home away from home), Vegan Represent.com, and VeggieBoards.com. Many areas also have regional boards as well, so you may find some locals with whom you can converse or even share a meal.

Kerry Casey

Business Name: Tattooedgeek, Inc.

Web Sites: www.mrstattooedgeek.etsy.com;
www.Homesweetveganhome.blogspot.com

What motivated you to start your business?

At Christmastime a few years back, I came across a news article reporting the horrific child labor conditions associated with a very well-known designer product. After reading this article, I found myself thinking about the products we buy and give as gifts, and specifically, the suffering, both human and animal, associated with these products. I couldn't shake my response to the stark contrast between how the products were created and how they were received in my mind.

I knew from that moment on that I wanted to create products which were created cruelty-free, from start to finish, that people could give as gifts. With that, Tattooedgeek was born.

Do you put an emphasis on the vegan aspect of the company, and, if so, do you find that it works in your favor?

Emphasizing that all of our products are vegan and cruelty-free has definitely proved to be very beneficial to our company. Declaring our products cruelty-free has sparked many conversations about how products other than food can be vegan. Our non-vegan customers are always surprised (and many are appalled)

when they hear about the multitude of possible ingredients a product can have that are derived from the exploitation of animals. I hope that our products appeal to all types of people with all types of personal beliefs; so far, I believe that they do. Let me tell you, vegans are some of the most loyal and supportive customers I have ever encountered. Tattooedgeek has been lucky enough to participate in several of the larger vending events held in the NYC area during the last few years. It didn't matter where the event was held or what the weather conditions were—vegans always come and shop for vegan products, and we love them for it!

Do you incorporate green practices into your work?

Tattooedgeek's goal is to create products that are cruelty-free, functional, affordable, and unique, with as little impact on our beautiful planet as possible. The core of our products is plant-based and completely sustainable. All of our printing is done on recycled paper, and all of our product containers are recyclable. Our commitment to our planet is never-ending; we are always in search of newer, more environmentally friendly ways to improve our products.

What's your favorite item that you sell?

While I enjoy the lip balms, fragrance, and jewelry, our soy candles are by far my favorite items to sell. Our customers have as much fun exploring our uniquely scented theme candles as I do designing them. The expression on a customer's face is priceless as they look over our candle line and discover the Zombie Love candle, or the El Luchador candle. As much as customers enjoy our candle graphics, what they find most impressive are the candle scents.

Erika Shuhendler

Business Name: Purrfect Pineapples

Web Site / Location: www.purrfectpineapples.com; Toronto, Ontario, Canada

What motivated you to start your business?

I have always loved lingerie and have never been satisfied with the fit or styles offered in the mall (i.e., not enough ruffles, bows were too small, bras didn't fit right, the rise of certain panties were awkward, etc.). I just always wanted to have a pair of panties where I could choose the color, cut, and style. Plus, lingerie is way more fun to sew than clothing is. You can make it so over the top that it's adorable, rather than tacky.

Do you put an emphasis on the vegan aspect of the company, and, if so, do you find it works in your favor?

Yes, I do. I advertise Purrfect Pineapples as "cruelty-free lingerie." I'm not sure if it works in my favor, but I try to make people aware that cruelty exists in fashion. You'd be surprised how many people don't think twice about wool or silk. I get a lot of questions about what "cruelty-free" means, especially at trade shows. That's why I make sure to keep a pile of Farm Sanctuary leaflets at my booth.

How do you handle any animosity toward veganism in your personal life or business?

I try to ignore it most of the time. People who are negative about veganism seem to never want to listen or understand it. If it's friends or family, I cook them a

nice vegan dinner and show them that vegan food is amazing—not just "rabbit food." Vegan Boston cream cupcakes generally change people's views.

Favorite vegan meal?

Kale salad, veggie lasagna, and pumpkin cheesecake for dessert!

DINING OUT!

While it's not likely you're going to have much success hitting the local fast-food joint or the mall food court, you can easily dine out vegan even if you don't have a vegetarian or vegan establishment in your area. A lack of a vegan restaurant doesn't mean you have to go to steakhouses and watch your friends eat flesh while you suffer through iceberg lettuce with no dressing and a plain baked potato. An easy way to satisfy all preferences and find a vegan option is to take a culinary trip around the world! Indian, Ethiopian, Thai, the Mediterranean, and other international regions of the world have many plant-based options that are suitable for vegans.

While some restaurants may know the word *vegan*, others won't, so be sure to check that they don't use ghee, butter, milk, egg noodles, fish sauce, or other animal-derived ingredients. Sometime the inclusion of a non-vegan ingredient that is not typical to a normally vegan dish will surprise you, so it is always best to ask questions. You'll also find that many restaurants will accommodate your needs, and some chefs will even enjoy the challenge of creating something for you if you're unable to order off the menu. Ideally, you should call these places in advance to make sure they can prepare something to avoid having a meltdown when you're stuck and hungry without food on your plate.

By dining at a non-vegan establishment, you're showing that there's a demand for vegan food, which could result in more options on the menu for everyone. Of course, since vegan food is suitable for everyone, remind your friends that next time, you should get to pick the restaurant; you might impress them with delicious options they've never tried before!

FIELDING PESKY QUESTIONS AND COMMENTS

It's bound to happen: Your oh-so-hilarious uncle will tell you he's a carnivore planning to eat the share of meat you won't, while your mom is afraid you're going to die from a lack of protein and won't stop asking questions. Don't panic, and don't get snarky! Whether it's curiosity or concern, they're talking about it for a reason, and you biting their heads off won't help anyone. Yes, it can be trying, but you always have the option to end the conversation. This is a life choice you've made, and you can either explain it calmly with people or just tell them that it is *your* choice, and you don't feel the need to discuss it.

Cuisine	Common Vegan Dishes	Things to Look Out For!
Indian / South Indian	Chana masala, aloo mutter, aloo gobi, dal, samosa, roti, chapati, pakora, paratha, saag, chole, dosa, uttapam, sambhar, idli	Ghee (especially in North Indian cuisine), milk, paneer (cheese), raita (yogurt sauce)
Italian	Spaghetti with tomato sauce, bruschetta, foccacia, minestrone soup, risotto, bread, pizza margherita sans cheese (the way it was originally made!)	Cheese, especially Parmesan, butter, cream or milk, meat sauce, animal stock, egg in fresh pasta
Mediterranean	Falafel, pita, hummus, baba ganoush, tabouli, lentil soup, ful mudammas, dolma	Egg, feta cheese, yogurt sauce
Thai / Chinese / Vietnamese	Stir-fry, noodles, rice Many of the dishes in Asian restaurants contain fish sauce, but can typically be made with other seasonings	Fish sauce, egg, egg noodles, chicken or beef broth, honey, dried shrimp
Japanese	Vegetable sushi, inari, soba and udon noodles, gyoza, daifuku, natto, umeboshi, onigiri, nori	Fish broth, dashi/bonito flakes, egg, even tofu can be cooked in fish, tempura batter (often contains egg), mayonnaise
Ethiopian	Wot or wett (sauces) and atkilts (vegetables), gomen, injera	Niter kebbeh (spiced butter)
Mexican / Latin	Vegetarian burritos and tacos sans queso and crema, beans, rice, guacamole, chips, fried Plantains	Cheese, sour cream, chicken or beef broth, lard

When you *do* choose to discuss your veganism with doubters, stay factual and explain your reasoning, and don't venture into gray areas. Some people are just looking to get a rise out of you with their MEAT IS TASTY FUCKING MURDER T-shirts. There's nothing better than being a level-headed and well-informed voice for veganism. Don't turn people off with a bad attitude; everyone has to start somewhere, and what led you to go vegan may not be the same motivator that would work for them!

HOLIDAYS, BIRTHDAYS, AND SPECIAL EVENTS

You may find that a carcass as the centerpiece of the table puts a damper on your holiday spirit, but you can build new traditions for yourself in order to be able to celebrate the holidays with your loved ones. Expecting others to successfully cater to you is a recipe for disaster, so plan on coordinating your meal options in advance. One great thing to do is to offer to bring a dish and a dessert, ensuring you'll have something to eat while introducing vegan food to the crowd. Everyone loves dessert! If your hosts insist on handling everything themselves, consider sending them some of your favorite recipes. Dishes like the Apple Sage Rice Stuffed Acorn Squash (recipe on page 166) appeal to everyone, as they don't scream "vegan," and they use ingredients commonly found in grocery stores.

Weddings can be a bit tougher, but luckily these days, caterers know there's bound to be a few vegetarians and people with allergies in the crowd. You may very well end up with the dreaded "GVP" (aka, the Grilled Vegetable Plate), with no sustenance in sight among the greasy limp slices of zucchini and overcooked bell peppers, but at least it's something, and you'll be happy you popped that Clif Bar in your bag to round out your meal. If you don't want to bring something to an event and nothing provided is suitable for you, do the age-old vegan trick: Eat before you get there! Don't be the starving vegan in the corner giving everyone else the evil eye. Have a meal beforehand, throw a snack in your bag if it's appropriate, and politely decline when your grandfather tries to pass you the turkey yet again.

On my first vegan Thanksgiving, my mother offered to make vegan mashed potatoes, I brought my own gravy and some seitan medallions, and the salad, green beans, and fruit kabobs were already veg-friendly, ensuring that I had a full plate to eat, just like everyone else. As the years have gone on, more and more dishes on the family table have become vegan, and there have even been a few all-vegan celebration meals. Your progress may vary, of course, but I certainly didn't make any by expecting everyone else to find something for me to eat. Sometimes it takes a while for your

loved ones to understand that it's not just a phase, and you're in this for the long haul, so be patient and kill 'em with kindness (along with tasty baked goods)!

THE VEGAN COMMUNITY: GET INVOLVED!

It can be rough being the lone vegan in your group of friends, but the good news is that most areas have at least a few vegans when you need like-minded company, and you may even find a new best friend! You're not going to know if you don't get out there and look, whether it's by checking the local co-op bulletin board or by scouring the Internet. A Google search can be a great resource for vegan message boards and blogs, as well as for local veg groups, and you can jump right in to get involved and attend events.

Activism

Activism is not only beneficial to the organization you're working with, but it can also be beneficial to your social life. Whether it's by leafleting or attending a rally or local board meeting, you'll have the opportunity to connect with like-minded individuals. Often a group of event participants will go out for a meal or drinks, so you can reward yourself for helping others while participating in great conversation. For more ideas on how to get involved, check out the Animal Activism section (see page 30).

Food Not Bombs

Food Not Bombs is a volunteer-run group that has been serving vegan and vegetarian food to the hungry for over thirty years. In over a thousand cities around the world, the meals are cooked in volunteers' kitchens, typically with donated food from local grocers. The food is then taken out to the public to feed the hungry and spread their message of peace. In my experience, it's been a fun challenge to see what will be donated that particular week, and to then come up with a meal off the cuff. It's like *Iron Chef* for vegans! Consider volunteering for your local chapter of Food Not Bombs, not only for the joy of cooking and the chance to serve those who are hungry, but also to ensure that people get a good cruelty-free meal that is helping to reduce the food waste in the world.

Blogs

When it comes to food blogs, vegans have certainly staked their claim on the Web. It seems like a new vegan blog pops up every day, and with blogging events like Vegan MoFo (the Vegan Month of Food), the vegan blog community continually expands to provide information and support. Blogs can be an invaluable place to find recipes, read product reviews, discover travel information, and even make new friends. My blog, The Urban Housewife, has been an integral part of my veganism, and has given me the opportunity to spread the word about important causes, to try new products, and to meet fabulous people all over the world. While you may not aspire to start your own blog, you can certainly participate by reading and commenting on others' blogs. I guarantee the writer will appreciate knowing that you read their entries!

Magazines

It's great to have some reading material you're excited about (other than your guilty pleasure, *Us Weekly*). Luckily, there are plenty of magazines for vegans, so you can have something by the toilet like everyone else. With vegan news, new product reviews, and recipes, *VegNews* brings all things vegan to your mailbox every other month. With an impressive cast of regular columnists and contributors who tackle the wide world of veganism, you'll find it hard to put this magazine down when it arrives. And environmentalists can rejoice, as *VegNews* also offers an eco-conscious tree-free edition of their magazine that can be purchased and downloaded from their Web site.

Vegetarian Times is a vegan-friendly publication and clearly marks which recipes are vegan, while many others are easily veganizable. The Vegetarian Resource Group offers up their publication, called *Vegetarian Journal*. In the UK, you'll find a quarterly publication called *Vegan* that includes recipes and articles, published by The Vegan Society.

Potlucks

Potlucks are a great way to bring people together, try new foods, and make friends. Vegans seem to have perfected the art of the potluck, as I've attended many successful events all over the world, with so much delicious food available that I didn't think I'd ever be able to eat again! Forums like the Post Punk Kitchen and Web pages like Meetup.com often coordinate potlucks, but it's also easy to organize your own. All you need is a location (typically, someone's house) and invitees, and with some local interest and word of mouth, the vegan food should come rolling in. Theme parties are a fun way to spice things up; I've been to "mini food" potlucks, sweets swaps, pizza parties, and even a Pee Wee Herman–themed potluck!

My first experience with a vegan potluck was when I was vegetarian. I saw a post on Yelp about a brunch potluck and decided to check it out. The Vegan Brunch Cartel was group of vegans, vegetarians, and even some omnivores in San Francisco who would get together once a month to share great food and conversation. The VBC gave me another push toward veganism, showing me that it was easy to make tasty vegan food. By the second or third potluck event, I was vegan, and I've never looked back. I know it influenced others to make a change in their diet as well. Never doubt the power of delicious, cruelty-free food!

VEGAN TATTOOS

Some of us vegans like to adorn ourselves in ink, but what you may not know is that not all tattoos are vegan. Tattoo inks can contain animal fat–based glycerin, while black ink can contain animal bones burned down to charcoal (called "bone char"). Luckily, there are vegan inks out there that are used by reputable artists, such as those produced by Eternal, Stable, and Classic. There are also tattoo ink brands with vegan colors, like Starbrite, Waverly, and Unique (although their black ink is not vegan). For black ink, Pelikan is suitable for vegans. Additionally, tattoo artists can make their own inks using pigment and vegetable-based glycerin. More and more tattoo artists are becoming aware of animal ingredients in tattoo ink, and there are even shops that only use vegan ink, like Scapegoat Tattoo in Portland, Oregon.

Other issues with tattooing can include preparation, cleaning, and aftercare. Before tattooing an area, the artist will remove the hair on the area to be tattooed, often with a razor that has an animal fat–based moisture strip. Opt for a razor without a moisture strip, or you may choose to bring your own. Green Soap, the industry-stan-

dard product used to clean off areas being tattooed, contains animal derivatives. Talk to your artist about using Dr. Bronner's or another suitable vegan option.

When healing a tattoo, A&D Ointment, Tattoo Goo, or Lubriderm lotion are often recommended, but these are not suitable for vegans. Products like Merry Hempsters Tattoo Balm, Stay True Organics, After Inked, and lotions that are unscented, lanolin-, and beeswax-free (from companies like Beauty Without Cruelty) are alternatives. With a bit of research, you can get a completely vegan tattoo, so now all you have to fear is getting the tattoo itself!

VEGAN COMPANION ANIMALS

A somewhat taboo subject among vegans is whether or not they should feed their companion animals a vegan diet. Canines are omnivorous, meaning that like humans, dogs can thrive on a plant-based diet. In fact, commercially available meat-based pet foods could be jeopardizing the health of your furry friend in the same way that humans eating meat are developing health issues. The four Ds—dead, dying, diseased, or disabled—describe the state of the animal flesh often used for pet food, while the foods also often contain pesticides, hormones, and antibiotics.

From pit bulls and Labrador retrievers to Lhasa apsos and pugs, dogs all over the world are living healthy lives on a vegan diet. My two-year-old Chihuahua, Strummer, has been vegan since she was a puppy, and she's happy and healthy. Many companies offer both wet and dry vegan dog foods, such as V-dog, Natural Balance, Natural Life, PetGuard, Ami Dog, Yarrah, and Evolution.

Another great option is to make your own food; companies like VegeDog offer supplements you can include to ensure that your canine is getting the right nutrients.

There are a plethora of treats available to keep your pooch happy as well. Buddy Biscuits and Dogswell Veggie Life Sweet Potato Chews are favorites in our house, and these days, even Trader Joe's has vegan dog treats! For other store-bought vegan dog treats, check out Boston Baked Bonz, Max & Ruffy's, Mr. Barky's, and Zuke's. Or, consider making your own treats from *The Simple Little Vegan Dog Book* by Michelle Rivera.

On the other hand, felines are carnivores, which makes a vegan diet difficult for cats. With cats, the biggest issue is taurine, which only occurs naturally in animal tissue (but has been produced synthetically since 1930). Many pet foods, both with and without meat, use synthetic taurine to meet nutritional requirements, but you still may find there are issues with a vegan diet for a carnivorous animal. One common suggestion is to feed your cats a partially vegan diet so as to reduce the suffering of animals, while making sure you are meeting your companion's dietary needs. I know people who have had success putting their cats on a 100 percent vegan diet, so do your research and decide what is best for you and your companion animal.

Other companion animals can include herbivorous animals like rabbits, birds, guinea pigs, and chinchillas. Some lizards, iguanas, and turtles are herbivorous as well. Many small animals end up in shelters, so when you're ready to add a new friend to your family, opt to rescue an animal in need rather than heading to the pet store.

Natural hygiene products are better for your companion animals, so when it's time for a bath or some oral care, opt for natural, chemical-free products from brands like Bark for Peace!, Buddy Rinse, earthbath, Orange Dog, Oxyfresh Pet Oral Hygiene Solution, Pet Organics, Rosie's Remedies, and Spot Organics.

Don't breed or buy while abandoned animals die! It seems so obvious, but many people forget about the millions of animals who are killed in shelters every year. While mutts are awesome, if you want a specific breed of companion animal, it's likely there is a rescue group in your area that specializes in that breed. Even if you don't find the perfect fit for your family right away, stay diligent and wait until the right option comes along. Breeders are not the answer, especially with the known genetic defects typically passed on through inbreeding, not to mention the rampant issues with puppy mills and backyard breeding. Animals in shelters need your help, so rescue one today and find your new best friend!

HIT THE ROAD: VEGAN TRAVEL IS EASY!

Anyone who knows me knows that I love to travel. If I could make a career out of discovering vegan food around the world and reporting on it, I most certainly would. Many people are concerned they'll be far from home and unable to find vegan fare, but I've found that to be very rare, so long as you're willing to do some research and planning before taking off to your destination. Resources like Happy Cow are invaluable because they provide veg options all over the world, often with reviews of various dining establishments. One thing to watch out for, however, are closures and incon-

sistencies in a restaurant's listed business hours. It's in your best interest to make sure a place is open and still in business before trekking out to it.

Yes, I said "trekking." While you can subsist on grocery-store bread rolls and peanut butter or eat your weight in falafel, the best vegan meals may be the ones you have to take a little journey to find. While I don't mind sitting on a train or bus to get to an establishment with an amazing specialty like vegan croissants, your travel partners may not feel the same way, so take that into consideration when making plans, and expect a bit of give-and-take. One thing I always do is bring a few snacks with me: Clif or Luna bars, seitan jerky, nuts, and dried fruit are great in case I need a quick fix and I don't know when I'll be sitting down for a meal with sufficient options, or when I can't get past the language barrier to find out what is vegan. Also, keep in mind that while airlines offer vegetarian nondairy meals (code VGML), they're not always entirely vegan, as they tend to have things like salad dressing with whey, unidentifiable margarine, and rolls with no ingredients listed on the package. That being said, the main dish is typically fine, and many times you'll be surprised by sweet treats like cookies or even donuts! The best part is being served your "special" meal first and finding that the people around you are envious because your meal looks and smells so much better than theirs!

MY FAVORITE CITIES FOR VEGAN GRUB

Ready to hit the road, but not sure where you want to go? If you're into a culinary adventure, the following cities have been more than kind to my taste buds!

New York City

Home to an all-vegan ice-cream parlor, and with everything from vegan Korean food to an organic chocolate shop, New York City rarely disappoints with its plethora of options. When I touch down in NYC, I know I'm in for two things: lots of walking and a full belly! SuperVegan.com is a great resource for all things vegan in NYC, and even has a mobile map feature built in, so you're never too far from something to nosh on.

Portland, Oregon

Often called the "vegan mecca," Portland offers everything from an all-vegan Italian restaurant, three vegan bakeries, an entirely vegan mini mall, and vegan-friendly food carts with $1 corn dogs, milkshakes, and fried hand pies. It seems you can't throw a stone without hitting a vegan or a vegan-friendly restaurant in PDX! For more on Portland vegan eats, check out StumptownVegans.com.

Los Angeles Area

From the Valley to Orange County, Southern California isn't lacking much in the vegan arena. Whether you want vegan chicken and waffles, an all-vegan pizza joint, an almond croissant, or a kale salad, you can find just about anything your heart desires, from healthy fare to greasy goodness. The only downside I've found is how spread-out everything is, making it difficult to maneuver without a car. Quarrygirl.com has the lowdown on the vegan-food scene in the land of sun and celebrities!

Berlin

Yes, Germany, the same country that brought us bratwurst! You'd be amazed at all the vegan eats available, from cupcakes and ice cream to a vegan version of the popular Döner kebab, and more variations on veggie burgers than you could ever dream up. They also have Veni Vidi Vegi, an all-vegan grocery shop, so you can stock up on delicious vegan gummies, pâtés, and chocolates without having to worry about reading unfamiliar labels!

Chicago

Even in the Midwest, there is an oasis of vegan options to be found in the Windy City! Perfect French toast, unbelievable pastries, and some of the best soul food you'll ever find are in Chicago. The famous Radical Reuben sandwich from The Chicago Diner is so amazing that even the Food Network has featured it. If that's not enough, it's also home to Chicago Soydairy, the makers of Dandies marshmallows, Temptation ice cream, and Teese Cheese, plus Upton's Naturals, purveyors of the perfect seitan!

San Francisco

Having lived in San Francisco for so many years, it's easy to take for granted the many vegan options, but the reality is that it's not lacking much! San Francisco is home to Millennium, one of the best vegan fine-dining spots in the world; all-vegan Japanese and Mexican restaurants; giant sub sandwiches; fully loaded ice-cream sundaes; and even multiple types of vegan donuts. Of course, it's also home to my vegan bakery, Sugar Beet Sweets, which I run with my good friends. We have you covered for all things sweet and delicious.

Danielle Distefano

Business Name: Only You Tattoo

Web Site / Location: www.onlyyoutattoo.com; Atlanta, Georgia

Do you put an emphasis on the vegan aspect of the company, and, if so, do you find that it works in your favor?

Yes, it has worked in my favor. Being vegan for almost fifteen years, and tattooing for nine, it tends to come up in conversations. Many of my clients respond positively to my choices, even if they are not vegan. They appreciate my complete understanding of my craft. It's not the main focus of my advertising, but it is an added incentive if you already like my work.

How do you handle any animosity toward veganism in your personal life or business?

I still get a little defensive about veganism because it's my lifestyle, and not just my diet of the week. I understand that people are set in their ways and can be closed-minded, so not pushing ideas onto others helps me get through to them. Easing them into veganism by pointing out things they already eat that just happen to be vegan can be a more-positive approach. Coming from a male-dominated and mostly meat-eating industry, I got picked on a lot, but you have to roll with the punches and be able to joke around. Things have changed a lot in ten years, and the word vegan is used more often in a positive light; however, there are still people that like to get a reaction out of you, so I have to choose my battles and not take everything so seriously.

What's your favorite tattoo you've done?

It's so hard to narrow it down to just one tattoo; a few that stick out over the years have been a unicorn throwing up a rainbow, and John Oates of Hall and Oates riding a unicorn. I have done a lot of vegan tattoos, and I really connect with them. I'm working on a big animal-liberation piece right now that definitely stands out.

Favorite vegan meal?

Okay, the serious stuff! I love food, so I have a few answers.

Breakfast: Vegan French toast from Pick Me Up Cafe in Chicago, and breakfast benedict from M Cafe in LA.

Lunch or dinner: Anything from Candle 79 in Manhattan, the best food I've ever had in my life.

My own cooked meal: Pesto tofu cashew cream stuffed shells with homemade marinara.

Desserts would be anything with chocolate, and carrot cake with cream cheese frosting!

ROOOOOAD TRIP!

While I'm not a fan of cars, sometimes they're a necessary evil in order to get from one place to another. When I'm in the car for hours at a time and need to stop at a gas station for a fill-up and some junk food, here's what you'll likely find headed back to the car with me:

Cracker Jack: Sweet caramel popcorn, roasted peanuts, and a toy surprise inside? Sign me up! These bring me back to the days of going to baseball games with my dad.

Fritos: Guaranteed to be made from non-GMO (genetically modified organism) corn, these crispy corn chips hit the spot when I need a salty fix. They also have other flavors that are vegan, although I can't vouch for the quality of the ingredients!

Sweet Tarts: Solid sugar discs in flavors like blue raspberry and grape. I can't begin to count the times we've been fueled by Sweet Tarts on a late-night drive. Made from all sorts of crap, sometimes you just have to throw caution to the wind and enjoy!

Nutter Butter: Crisp, peanut-shaped cookies filled with uber-sweet peanut-butter filling and lord knows what else, but they sure are tasty! "Pre-gan," my husband ate these all the time, and when he found out they're vegan, he was

stoked—although they're just an occasional treat these days.

Red Vines: When they're fresh, they're soft and chewy. When they're not fresh, they're solid as a rock, but somehow still delicious. Is "red" the flavor of these licorice vines? I don't know; but I do know they're perfect for chowing down at the movies, or maybe even as a substitute drinking straw from time to time.

Mel

Location: Oakland, California

Blog: veglicious! (veglicious.blogspot.com)

Favorite Dish to Cook: Pho and Sunday-night pizza!

Favorite Vegan Hater Comeback: "You say you care, but that's a lie. My true compassion is for all living things, and not just the ones that are cute!"

Funniest Vegan Moment: The first vegan cake I ever made was ambitious: two layers of vanilla cake with strawberry frosting. I'm not sure where I went wrong, but the thing weighed about 25 pounds, tasted like pure baking soda, and after a night in the fridge, had a frosting vs. cake chemical reaction that turned a 1/4-inch layer of the cake blue-gray anywhere it touched the frosting.

Jen Fosnight

Business Name: Never Felt Better by Jen

Web Site / Location: www.neverfeltbetterbyjen.com; Sacramento, California

Do you put an emphasis on the vegan aspect of the company, and, if so, do you find that it works in your favor?

*I do! Shortly after making the decision to a) have my own business, and b) become vegan, we moved to Portland, Oregon, which made both ideals come to "real life." Portland has vibrant and active crafting and vegan communities, so blending the two seemed natural. I thought it was essential for people to know that I didn't use animal products in my work, and, more important, **why** I didn't. I found a lot of support in*

the vegan community and made a lot of contacts and friends.

Since then we have relocated to Sacramento, and there is even more need for me to identify myself as vegan artist. Every single craft show I do is an opportunity to educate about veganism, and I have never regretted the decision to put so much emphasis on being a vegan crafter and business owner. It sets me apart and allows me to help the animal rights movement all at the same time.

What's the most rewarding part of running a vegan business?

The outreach and the community; the sense of well-being it promotes by simply doing what's right makes the nuts and bolts of the "business" seem easy. It's rewarding to see that "aha" moment on

the face of someone who previously hadn't known a thing about what's really going on with their "food supply." Veganism isn't hard at all . . . It's honestly the easiest thing I have ever done. That's part of the fun in my business name, "Never Felt Better," because I truly have never been this at peace before. I know that what I am doing is exactly right.

Do you incorporate green practices into your work?

I recycle, repurpose, and reuse pretty much everything! I use vintage and thrifted fabrics, eco-felt (made from plastic bottles), and things that are gifted and passed along to me. I find great pleasure in turning found objects into something cute and cruelty-free!

When you're not working, what do you like to do?

I love to cook and eat delicious vegan food. My husband and I have started a local vegan eating guide blog, and I am working on a small vegan cookzine to pass along some of my better recipes from over the years. I love to thrift-shop for treasures and fabrics. I have two daughters and a stepdaughter who keep my husband and me busy. We have two dog and two cat companions whom we love very much. I also nanny a three-year-old for a vegan woman who runs the only vegan café in town.

I have to give a vegan shout-out to my husband Shawn, for his patience with me and all of my dumb questions when we first met. A vegan for twenty years, Shawn has guided me on my vegan path. He's an amazing partner!

Karla Hansen

Business Name: Tattooing—The Anchored Soul; Sewing—Geek Freeks and Kraftbomb

Web Site / Location: www.theanchoredsoul.com; Auckland, New Zealand, www.kraftbomb.com; www.geekbooteek.blogspot.com

What motivated you to start your business?

With my tattooing, I was trained by the late Phill Matthias, and his faith in me is what has motivated—and still motivates me today—to tattoo people. As far as the sewing, it was really my husband's fault; he is an animator and got really inspired by seeing the plush movement overseas. He thought, "Hey, my amazing wifey can sew; we should do that!" When my friend City and I created Kraftbomb, it was a case of "There are so many amazing crafters and no regular outlet . . . Let's start our own regular market! Okay!"

Do you put an emphasis on the vegan aspect of the company, and, if so, do you find that it works in your favor?

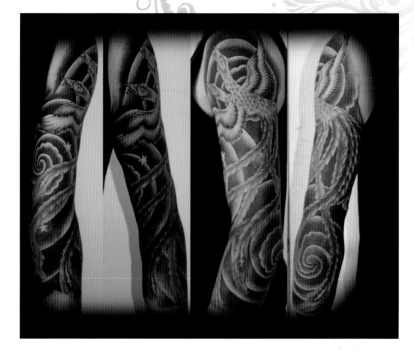

As far as tattooing goes, I do use vegan ink, and when people know that, they are usually happily surprised. With Kraftbomb we host the Worldwide Vegan Bake Sale every year, which works in our favor because it brings in people who possibly haven't heard of Kraftbomb, or wouldn't ordinarily come to other events.

What's the most rewarding part of running a vegan business?

I guess it's the same as making the choice in your personal life to be vegan—it's completely liberating and satisfying just knowing that you are doing all that you can in each and every little way.

When you're not working, what do you like to do?

When I'm not tattooing, I am always sewing and also hanging at home with my husband and cats.

Killing an animal to make a coat is sin. It wasn't meant to be, and we have no right to do it. A woman gains status when she refuses to see anything killed to be put on her back. Then she's truly beautiful.
—Doris Day

CHAPTER 4

SHOPPING LIKE A VEGAN WHEN YOU'RE NOT BUYING FOOD

While it may seem like food is the focal point of veganism, there is more to consider if you want to live a cruelty-free lifestyle. Leather, fur, wool, silk, and down are just some of the materials that exploit animals in the name of fashion or furnishings. Additionally, animal testing for beauty products is still happening around the world.

Pleather, Not Leather

It's a myth that leather is always a by-product of the meat industry, but in many cases wearing leather supports factory farming. Much like factory farming, the animals endure horrible conditions and are typically raised in countries with zero (or very few) animal-welfare laws, in many cases making it legal to skin them alive. While people fawn over soft leather, softness means that the animal was young and likely a dairy industry by-product. In some cases the skin may come from the unborn baby of a slaughtered mother.

Cows are not the only animal being used for their skin, as leather can also be made from pigs, goats, sheep, alligators, ostriches, and kangaroos. In some countries, dogs and cats are slaughtered for their meat and skins. It's almost impossible to find out the source of your leather, as it's rarely labeled.

Michelle Schwegmann

Business Name: The Herbivore Clothing Company
Web Site / Location: www.herbivoreclothing.com; 1211 S. E. Stark Street, Portland, Oregon

What motivated you to start your business?

When I went veg, I was so excited about it, I wanted to fly the flag with a T-shirt—but there was nothing out there that I would even consider wearing. I wanted good design, clever thoughts, and fashionable styles, so my husband and I started Herbivore.

Do you put an emphasis on the vegan aspect of the company, and, if so, do you find that it works in your favor?

*Our company is rooted in veganism, so it's more than just an aspect of our business—it **is** our business. We have become an information source for people in the community, and for new vegans and vegetarians espe-*

cially. Our goal is to make veganism the normal way to be, to show its benefits and how easy and fun and sensible it is . . . and how it's cool, too. Being thoughtful and intelligent and caring is amazingly cool.

How do you handle any animosity toward veganism in your personal life or business?

I know that animosity stems from ignorance and fear. Once a person isn't threatened by me or by veganism—I've found that it's hard to be threatened by me, but veganism sure threatens a lot of folks—they are more likely to open their mind to the idea that someone else's veganism isn't a direct threat to them personally. Usually I ignore the jerks.

What's the most rewarding part of running a vegan business?

I answer to my own conscience and get to help a lot of people and a lot of animals!

PVC is hardly environmentally sustainable, but is it worse than exploiting animals? It's a dilemma, and it's up to you to decide how you feel about it, although there are PVC alternatives. Products like Matt & Nat's handbags and olsen Haus shoes are made from ethically sourced and recycled leather-like materials that are far better for the environment. Of course, you can also just stick to all-natural fibers like hemp!

Faux, Not Fur

It amazes me that there are still people out there who wear the fur of animals. Sure, it's no different than leather, but fur is taboo even to non-vegetarians. From the videos showing foxes being skinned alive, to the discovery that coats can have hoods lined with dog fur (which is obviously not marked as such), it's pretty safe to say there's nothing ethical about fur, no matter where you live. Recently, a cryptically hilarious "Fur is Green" campaign was launched by the Fur Council of Canada, claiming fur to be a renewable source that's environmentally friendly. Really? Animals are renewable? I like to wear an anti-fur pin in the winter to remind people that it's neither fashionable nor kind to torture animals for their hides. Some people opt to wear faux fur, which has made leaps and bounds and can look authentic these days. The issue some see with this is you're making the hide of an animal seem like a fashion statement and people may not realize it is faux. This is one of those gray areas; you have to decide how you approach it.

The Woes of Wool

Many people are confused when it comes to wool, since the animal is shaved and not killed. While I don't believe humans should use animals for any products, there's still the cruelty issue at hand. Domesticated sheep have been bred to produce more wool, which means they require frequent shaving so they will not suffer from heat exhaustion, or have flies laying eggs in their skin (hatched eggs means flies will eat them alive). In order to prevent this process, called *fly strike*, farmers will cut large strips of skin from the buttocks and around the tail of the sheep, without anesthesia, a practice called *mulesing*.

As if the cruelty of mulesing isn't enough, many sheep are often sheared before they would naturally shed their coats, causing them to die of exposure to the cold.

Additionally, sheep are often packed tightly into trucks without food or water, or into holding pens where many are trampled, or get sick and die. At this stage, many sheep will have their throats slashed and be left to die a slow and painful death. With all of the alternative materials out there to keep you warm, how could anyone choose to wear wool?

Other "Wools" to Look Out For

Although we often think of wool as coming from sheep, there are a number of similar fibers that come from other animals that are often harvested in a similarly cruel fashion. If you see any of the following terms on a clothing label, you will know it came from an animal: merino, llama, vicuña/vicugna, angora, alpaca, cashmere, and mohair.

Silk

Much as a spider spins a web, silk is excreted by the silk-moth larva in order to bind itself into a cocoon during its fragile pupal state. Because silk is what is called a monofilament—that is, each cocoon consists of one long, single strand—harvesting silk always means killing the pupa before it matures and chews its way out of the cocoon. The silk filament is kept tightly bound in a cocoon shape by the saliva of the silk-moth pupae. In order to harvest a single monofilament from each cocoon, the saliva is dissolved by immersing the cocoons in boiling water. That's right; the larvae are boiled alive, like lobsters. An added element of cruelty to the silk industry is that many silk-fiber producers use child labor and/or unsafe harvesting practices. Some videos of silk-harvesting operations show school-aged children dipping their bare hands into scalding water to catch silk filaments as they unwind from the cocoons.

VEGAN FABRIC ALTERNATIVES BY ERIKA LARSON

Natural Fibers

Cotton

Cotton is an incredibly versatile fiber that grows on plants. It can be spun very fine to make the lightest and sheerest of summer blouses; it can be made into the denim of your favorite pair of jeans; or it can be woven into a thick canvas to make sneakers or a heavy-duty work coat. Cotton keeps the wearer either cool or warm, wicks moisture away from the skin, and is extremely low-maintenance; no dry-cleaning is necessary for this common fiber. The pesticides and fertilizers used in the cotton industry are a significant factor in agricultural pollution, however, so make an effort to buy organically farmed cotton whenever available or possible.

Linen

Sometimes called jute, linen comes from the reed-like flax plant and is a wonderful warm-weather fiber. Cool and light, linen cloth has a wonderfully "springy" texture. It can also be incorporated into heavy-duty fabrics.

Other plant-based fibers

As sustainability grows in importance among consumers and designers, and as previously localized products find their way around the globe, a growing interest in previously "exotic" plant fibers is finding its way into stores. Banana, which behaves much like linen; hemp, which struggles against associations with marijuana despite its durability, versatility, and sustainability; and bamboo, which boasts a delightful luster, robust softness, and quick growing cycle, are all examples of some of the alternative plant fibers you can expect to see showing up in your local clothing store.

Synthetic Fibers

Acrylic

Acrylics have come a long way over the past several decades. Modern textile designers create fibers that replicate the shape of wool fibers with a polymer base. As a result, acrylic mimics the warmth and wind resistance of wool, but without that scratchy feeling.

Polyester

It's not just for leisure suits anymore. Like other synthetic fibers, the technology around polyester has advanced to the point where this durable and versatile fiber can mimic the cotton jersey of a T-shirt, the satiny luster of a silk gown, and the tough twill of a woolen pea coat.

Rayon

Rayon is a unique fiber in that it's a little bit human-made, but also somewhat natural. Unlike other synthetic fibers that are made from polymer, rayon is made from wood pulp. The fibers are extracted through a "spinnerette" (imagine a showerhead with fibers coming out instead of water). As a result, rayon wears like linen but can be manipulated as it is extracted to create a variety of textures and properties.

Other animal-based materials to watch out for include down, ivory, pearl, mohair, snakeskin, tortoiseshell, angora, camel hair, and bone.

PREVIOUSLY OWNED, VINTAGE, AND SECONDHAND ITEMS

While I can't condone the use of animal products—whether or not you owned them before you went vegan, or bought them secondhand—there are people who do use items until they wear out, or who would rather use a secondhand item so it's at least fully used before ending up in a landfill. You have to decide on your own personal comfort level. Some people just don't have the financial means to throw out "pre-gan" clothing, and there's nothing wrong with that. When it comes to second-hand non-vegan items, you can choose not to buy them. One issue you may consider is that it reinforces the idea that animal products are considered fashionable, which can contribute to the further purchase of said items. Again, it's something you have to decide for yourself.

CRUELTY-FREE FASHION

Want to support businesses with 100 percent vegan goods and look stylish at the same time? Check out these companies for cruelty-free fashion!

Shoes

Beyond Skin, Bourgeois Boheme, Charmone Shoes, Cri de Coeur, Hydra Heart, Kailia Footwear, Keep Shoes, Melissa Plastic Dreams, Mink Shoes, Mohop Shoes, NAH, Neuaura Shoes, Novacas, olsen Haus, Ragazzi Vegan, SMARTFISH Handmade Footwear, The Generation, Vegetarian Shoes, Wicked Hemp

Purses and Accessories

amykathryn Handbags, Cherry Berry Handbags, English Retread, Jaan J., Matt & Nat, Melie Bianco, NOAH Handbags, NOHARM, Pansy Maiden, Queen Bee Creations, Snooty Jewelry, Splaff, Susan Nichole Handbags, The Vegan Collection, Truth Belts, Vegan Queen, Vegan Wares

Elizabeth Olsen

Business Name: olsen Haus: Pure Vegan
Web Site / Location: www.olsenhaus.com; New York City

What motivated you to start your business?

As a young child I was aware that there was something very wrong in the relationship between humankind and the animal kingdom. When I was fifteen, I saw some PETA literature and instantly became a vegetarian. I remained one for nineteen years; then, about three years ago, I put two and two together in regard to the dairy industry, and I went vegan. Being in the fashion industry for many years, I realized there weren't really any companies making good-quality and stylish vegan footwear and other products. The synthetic shoes available were not only cheap and hurt my feet, but they were not really designed, but rather copied from other designers. I knew that the way they were made was incongruent with the principles I value in my life.

The creation of olsen Haus was about filling this need, but even more important, I wanted it to be a vehicle to expose the truth about how animals are treated, the horrors of the leather industry, and the damage it does to the environment. I wanted to show that someone could be conscious of these things and still lead a fabulous lifestyle; I also wanted to emphasize how all living beings are linked, and that vegans could still have rad shoes.

Another mission in starting the company was to change the face/perception of what it means to be vegan. True creativity, style, and design are not synonymous with cruelty, and I want to enable consumers to make ethical choices when it comes to choosing stylish, fashionable products. Being vegan isn't about lack of style; it's actually about creativity and choosing a cruelty-free lifestyle.

Do you put an emphasis on the vegan aspect of the company, and, if so, do you find that it works in your favor?

Absolutely. I made a decision in the beginning to truly get the word out fast: I would have to be true to myself and the animals about why yet another shoe company was being created, so the words PURE VEGAN *are in the logo, and on every product. It was a risk, but it was the best decision I ever made. It has not hurt my business or exposure one bit; in fact, I believe that one reason why people all over the globe are drawn to my company is that they subconsciously know it's the right path, and they are curious. Members of the media have shown interest since day one, and we have appeared in hundreds of magazines, Web press pieces, and on television.*

I also put information and disturbing photos about the industry on the Web site—not for shock value, but to be true to the product and to show what is really happening. I have nothing to hide, but the industry as a whole has everything to hide. If you eat meat and wear leather, fur, wool, or silk, you are contributing to this.

Do you incorporate green practices into your work?

Well, first and foremost, I am vegan, which has the largest impact on the environment. I try to work with as many vegan professionals as possible. Everyone who is a regular business associate is vegan, or on their way! We do all the usual stuff—recycle; do everything electronically and paper-free; reuse boxes and packing materials. The product for Fall 2010 is made of recycled industrial waste from television screens, with details in the collection using recycled rubber tires for soling, and sustainable materials like wood and cork. I am also working on a heel made of recycled plastic bottles.

Melanie Pyves

Location: Toronto, Ontario, Canada

Blog: The Streets I Know: A Vegan Fashion Blog (streetsiknow.blogspot.com)

When did you become interested in fashion, and why did you start your blog?

I've been interested in fashion since I was a teenager. I collected teen fashion magazines and I had a sketchbook full of my own fashion illustrations. I wanted to be a fashion designer on and off throughout high school. Meanwhile, I also wanted to be a veterinarian. I currently work as a graphic designer by day and a fashion blogger by night.

I started my vegan fashion blog because after I had finally mastered the diet part of being vegan, I realized it was time for me to focus on making the other parts of my life cruelty-free. For me, that meant learning how to veganize my wardrobe, accessories, and beauty products. So, like most people in this day and age, I went online to find answers. I discovered tons of fabulous vegan clothing, shoes, purses, bags, hats, belts, and beauty products; I found whole fashion lines that were vegan and cruelty-free.

However, what I didn't find was a blog or Web site dedicated solely to sharing this fabulous information with other fashion-seeking vegans. Yes, there were a few blogs that were sharing some vegan fashion information here and there, but for me, that was not enough. I felt there needed to be a blog/site that was dedicated to just vegan and cruelty free fashion, and so that is how The Streets I Know: A Vegan Fashion Blog came about. I created it from my love for vegan fashion, and my need to share that love with other vegan-fashion enthusiasts. I also really wanted to help people see that it is possible and easy to be compassionate about fashion.

What do you find is the biggest misconception about vegan fashion?

That vegan fashion is boring and ugly. Okay, maybe that was true ten or fifteen years ago, but today, it is possible to be a very fashionable vegan. Vegan fashion lines like olsen Haus: Pure Vegan, Matt & Nat, Vaute Couture, Stella McCartney, Everyday Apparel, and so many more are making it possible. If you want to be a cruelty-free fashionista, you can be! Vegan fashion is really amazing right now; no matter what your style is, there is a vegan-fashion option out there that will help you express it.

Are you finding that more mainstream lines are making vegan pieces?

Yes; I see this mostly in shoes. There seem to be a lot of sites for mainstream brands that will have a section dedicated to vegan shoes. Simple, Macbeth, Chinese Laundry, and Irregular Shoes are a few brands that come to mind. There are also a lot of companies that are making vegan bags/purses too.

Who are your favorite designers / fashion lines?

Melissa Plastic Dream Shoes, Vaute Couture, Everyday Apparel, olsen Haus: Pure Vegan, Pansy Maiden, SMARTFISH Footwear, Beyond Skin, Keep Shoes . . . I could go on and on and on. Just head on over to my blog and see what I'm posting, because it will most likely show what my current favorite is.

Apparel

April77, Autonomie Project, Everyday Apparel, Healing Heart Designs, Herbivore Clothing, Lion's Share Industries, Model Citizen Clothing, Purrfect Pineapples, Secret Society of Vegans, Sick On Sin, Tippitappi, Trash Rags, Vaute Couture, Vegetable Slut

Mail-Order and Boutiques

All Vegan, Alternative Outfitters, Cow Jones Industrials, Ethique Nouveau, Fast and Furless, Herbivore Clothing, Humanitaire, Karmavore, MooShoes, Muso Koroni, Neon Collective, Panacea, Pangea, The Chocolate Shoe Box, Vegan Essentials, Vegans Love Lava, Viva Granola Vegan Store

Cruelty-Free Clothing Blogs and Web Sites

Animal Friendly Shopping, Chic Vegan, Compassionate Fashion, Girlie Girl Army, The Discerning Brute, The Professional Vegan, The Streets I Know, Shoes with Souls, Vegan Kicks, Vegan Shoe Addict, Veggie Shoe, What I Wore, you are an animal.

VEGAN BEAUTY

Sacrificing or torturing animals in the name of vanity is never beautiful. Luckily, there are plenty of options out there for the cruelty-free gal—without animal fat or ground-up beetles hiding inside the products. No longer are we relegated to just henna hair dye and patchouli soap! With the organic market expanding, many of the new beauty lines being developed are plant-based, and are marking their products *vegan* to appeal to the wider market. Additionally, products that were already vegan are being marked as such, and some lines are even changing ingredients to make items vegan-friendly.

You don't have to have a Whole Foods in town to find natural beauty products. Sure, a co-op or even a Trader Joe's would be nice, but even drugstores are starting to stock a wider selection of vegan products these days. Mail-order can also be a great option, although it can be a bit tougher to make returns, if needed.

With blogs like Vegan Beauty Review, you can keep track of the latest and greatest in vegan products, and a quick Google search of an item will likely yield answers about its ingredients. Rather than send you out into the world looking for a new beauty routine, I thought I would list some of the companies who make vegan-friendly products. Also, Sunny from Vegan Beauty Review, a gal who's tried more vegan cosmetics than we could count, has shared her Top 10 Vegan Beauty Products, as have I!

ANIMAL TESTING VS. ANIMAL INGREDIENTS

While NO ANIMAL TESTING labels run rampant on everything from shampoo to eyeliner these days, unfortunately, there are still animal-derived ingredients to look out for. This label does not mean that a product is cruelty-free; it only means that the product was not tested on animals. While an extensive list of companies who do not test on animals is easily found online, vegan-specific products can be a bit tougher to find, so be sure to check the ingredients. If you're not sure, try an online search, or e-mail the company for an answer. Web sites CrueltyFreeFace.com and VeganBeautyReview.com can also give you a nudge in the right direction. Don't be afraid to share your newly found vegan product with the rest of us! Post it on a message board, Twitter, or anywhere else you think others may find this information valuable.

Animal-Based Ingredients in Beauty Products

While this is hardly a complete list, here are some common animal products found in cosmetics. (You'll find many ingredients have similar names to these, which can also be animal-derived. Additionally, synthetic or vegetable versions may be used, so check the source of the ingredient by contacting the company who manufactures the product in question.)

Acetate*, allantoin*, ambergris, amino acids*, amylase, beeswax, biotin*, carmine, carminic acid, casein, castoreum, cera alba*, cetyl alcohol, cochineal, collagen, elastin, gelatin, glycerin*, guanine, honey, hyaluronic acid, hydrolyzed animal or milk protein, isopropyl lanolate, keratin, lactose, lanolin, lecithin*, mink oil, musk, ribonucleic acid (RNA)*, royal jelly, silk powder, stearic acid*, squalene*, tallow, urea*, vitamin A*, vitamin D3. (Items marked with an asterisk may come from a synthetic or vegetable source.)

Makeup Brushes

These can be made from either animal hair or synthetic materials, such as nylon or polyester. Unfortunately, the more commonly used source is hair from squirrels, badgers, ponies, weasels, or goats. The good news is that lines like Urban Decay, Aveda, Advanced Beauty Tools, Crown Brush, Furless Vegan Makeup Brushes, and EcoTools have a full range of synthetic Taklon brushes that are just as good (if not better) than the hairy versions. As a makeup artist myself, I use plenty of synthetic brushes with excellent results, and most cosmetics lines have at least a few in their repertoire, if you can't find an entirely vegan line.

Top 10 Vegan Beauty Products, by Sunny Subramanian of Vegan Beauty Review

Sunny Subramanian is editor in chief and writer for Vegan Beauty Review (www. veganbeautyreview.com), where you can read all the latest reviews about cruelty-free, organic, and green beauty products, fashion, food, and everything else vegan. Her goal is to show the world that being vegan can be fun and beautiful!

I've been a compassionate beauty junkie for as long as I can remember. I feel very lucky that there are a plethora of vegan beauty options that cover the gamut of all our vegan beauty needs. Whether you're in the market for cruelty-free makeup, organic and vegan body lotions, or all-natural facial cleansers, the world is your proverbial oyster. Here's a list of some of the favorite vegan beauty products that I've become smitten with over the years. They are in no particular order, but they are all particularly awesome:

1) **Crazy Rumors Lip balm**

These lip balms are 100 percent vegan and come in really fun and tasty flavors: Fresh Squeezed, A La Mode, Brew, Perk, Gumball, and Candy Cane—I highly recommend them all! They are the perfect consistency—not oily, lumpy, or sticky—and they are packed with moisturizing ingredients like jojoba oil, organic shea butter, extra virgin olive oil, and vitamin E. They are also naturally sweetened with stevia. My faves are Amaretto and Orange Bergamot.

2) **Strawberry Hedgehog Soaps**

This small business is run by the multitalented Tracy, who makes soap and jewelry and also blogs. She is a genuine sweetheart who crafts the most amazing-smelling soaps, body creams, and lip balms on the planet. She uses 100 percent pure and organic ingredients, and all of her products are like exceptional, masterful art pieces—they are simply gorgeous to look at, beautifully smelling, and effective to boot. Her line of soap scents constantly changes with each season, but some of my faves include Juniper Berry and Pure Lavender.

3) **Giovanni Hair Care**

This is a nourishing hair-care line that is of salon quality; the products smell amazing and are super-effective. They have different formulas for all hair types and hair-care needs. This line is quite accessible and is available at Target. I've tried many a vegan, hippie shampoo, but this hair-care line is far from typically hippie; it's comparable to traditional shampoos and conditioners except that it's even better, as it's primarily vegan (some products contain honey), organic, and cruelty-free. A couple of my faves are the Tea Tree Triple Treat Shampoo and their Smooth as Silk Shampoo.

4) **Urban Decay**

It's nice to be able to walk into Sephora and not feel like a complete outsider. There usually aren't many vegan options at giant makeup stores, but thank goodness for brands like Urban Decay. They have many vegan options, which include eye shadows and lip glosses that are fun, glittery, and high-quality, with dense pigmentation. Look for Marley's purple paw print on their Web site, which is placed next to all makeup products that are vegan.

5) **Dazzle Dry**

This vegan, nontoxic, and effective nail system incorporates nail prep, a base coat, nail lacquer, and a top coat—all of which are fast-drying and chip-resistant.

6) **LUSH**

Bath time can be vegan, sexy, and fun, all at the same time. LUSH has a line of vegan bubble bars, bath bombs, lotions; you name it! I highly recommend the Sex Bomb and their glittery bubble bars. They also donate money to a range of environmental and animal-friendly charities.

7) **Dr. Bronner's Castile Soaps**

Dr. Bronner might seem like an eccentric hippie, but he certainly knows a thing or two about soaps. Dr. Bronner's Castile Soaps are extremely versatile and can be used around the house for all of your cleaning needs (i.e., laundry, dog bath, body wash, dishwasher soap, car wash, etc.). These eco-friendly soaps come in a variety of scents: peppermint (my fave), eucalyptus, almond, rose, citrus, tea tree, and lavender.

8) **Original Sprout Detangler**

This product has saved many a hair on my delicate head. My hair is wavy and fine, and thus mega susceptible to frizziness and tangles. Luckily products like these are around to save the day. I *love* this detangler! This particular product is light, moisturizing, and frickin' kicks ass. It does an amazing job at leaving my hair soft, clean, and manageable. It works immediately and allows me to comb my hair effortlessly. This is by far the best detangler I have ever used to date.

9) **Be Fine Food Skin Care**

All of their products are made from popular fruits, grains, and veggies that we all love like beets, coconuts, rice, almonds, mushrooms . . . you could basically eat this line of skin care (but don't)! Their products are affordable and are even available at drugstores (i.e., Rite Aid and CVS). This beauty line is very effective, and they have products for every skin type. I highly recommend their Warming Clay Mask and Mint Gentle Cleaner.

10) Frais Hand Sanitizer

This organic hand sanitizer contains an alcohol concentration of 66 percent pure sugarcane, and has a natural blend of essential oils that help moisturize your skin so it stays soft and smooth. This sugarcane alcohol uses up to 10 percent less energy than typical corn alcohol, so it's more environmentally sound, and hey, I'm a fan of anything made from sugar! This hand sanitizer, which smells like fruits and herbs, is far from obnoxious, and it's also very effective.

MY TOP 10 VEGAN BEAUTY PRODUCTS

I spent ten years as a makeup artist working in print and production work, building up a kit of amazing products from lines both big and small. When I went vegan, some of the products had to get the boot, but I went out and found great vegan replacements; often, the products were even better than what I'd been using before! This inspired me to launch CrueltyFreeFace.com, so I could share my knowledge with others. If you walked in my house right now, you would find each and every one of these items:

1) Obsessive Compulsive Cosmetics

OCC is a 100 percent vegan line created for makeup artists, meaning you'll find only the highest-quality, well pigmented products in their range. From airbrush makeup for the pros to nail polish in every shade, you'll likely find what you're looking for. Their critically acclaimed Lip Tar is remarkable, and comes in every color of the rainbow, from nude all the way to black. These babies are so pigmented, you only need a drop for your entire lips! I'm a hot-pink lips kind of gal, so you'll find me rockin' Anime or Pageant lip tars, which have phenomenal staying power, so I don't have to reapply all day.

2) Pureology

A staple in salons, this sulfate-free shampoo and conditioner line will put your hair in the best shape of your life. All Pureology products, including their awesome styling line, are vegan, so shop with confidence and get ready for great hair! While the products are not inexpensive, they tend to last a long time, and are definitely worth the price. I use the PureVolume system, along with a few different styling products based on my hair mood, with great results. I cannot live without Pureology!

3) **Sugarpill Cosmetics**

While I have known Amy from Sugarpill since we were both in high school and going to ska shows at teen centers, I am one picky gal when it comes to eye shadow, and no friendship could change that. Sugarpill has a beautiful range of highly pigmented loose shadows, all of which are vegan. My favorites include Goldilux, Hysteric, and Starling. In addition to the loose shadows, they also have a gorgeous vegan deep purple pressed shadow called Poison Plum. Due to carmine, purple vegan shadows are hard to find, but thankfully we have Sugarpill to fill that gap!

4) **Urban Decay**

A longtime staple in my kit has been Urban Decay cosmetics, and not just because they gave me a ton of free makeup when I worked on the Heatherette show at Fashion Week. Shopping for Urban Decay is easier than ever these days, with vegan options denoted by a purple paw print on the item, and even their Web page has a marked vegan section. One of my favorite items is Love Junkie XXX Shine lip gloss, a deeply colored but very sheer plum gloss that suits everyone and looks great over lipstick, or on its own. They also have excellent lid primer, eye shadows, and all vegan makeup brushes.

5) **ZuZu Luxe**

ZuZu Luxe offers a full range of all-vegan cosmetics, found in many health stores as well as online. While I can't vouch for the color line, I regularly use their Undereye Concealer and Dual Powder Foundation, with great results. Additionally, finding good mascara can be tough, but ZuZu Luxe black mascara is my go-to for flirty lashes. The trick is to scrape the excess mascara off the wand along the top of the tube before applying, so you don't end up with clumpy spider lashes . . . unless you're into that sort of thing!

6) **Special Effects Hair Dye**

Sometimes you want to get a little loud with your hair color; thankfully, we have Special Effects. No need to worry about questionable ingredients, as this line is cruelty-free! From Hi-Octane Orange to Joyride Purple, all shades of the rainbow are covered, and some even glow under a black light! Atomic Pink and I have had an on-again, off-again relationship for years, and while we're currently off, I suspect it won't be long before it comes back into my life.

7) Spa Ritual Nail Polish

I can't seem to keep a manicure for more than five minutes, but Spa Ritual nail polish has a lasting power I've never experienced before. Available in a wide range of nail salons, these Dibutyl Phthalate (DBP), formaldehyde-, and toluene-free polishes come in an awesome range of colors. My favorite shade at the moment is a hot-pink number called Love; it's what I'm wearing on the book cover!

8) Hair Fix

When you color your hair, the last thing you want to do is wash it every day and allow your color to fade. Enter dry shampoo! Hair Fix is a vegan-owned company, and their range of dry shampoos makes my oily hair look freshly washed and smelling great, meaning I can preserve my color and spend less time in the bathroom. Made from a blend of starches, this product attacks the problem at the source—the roots! The company recently added lip balms and soap to their line, so look out for those as well (I've been enjoying the pomegranate lip balm, myself).

9) ShiKai

This California-based vegan company makes everything from shampoo and body wash to skin-care and styling products. I currently use their Borage Eye Cream to keep the skin under my eyes lush and hydrated, and in the past I have also used their face wash and facial lotion, as well. A staple in our house is their moisturizing shower gel (Yuzu—a lovely Japanese citrus scent) to help us wake up in the morning, and I often have a sample-size hand cream in my purse. Did I mention I use the Color Reflect shampoo to keep my hair color bright, too?

10) Merry Hempsters

While I shied away from hemp products for years, buying in to the stereotype that they're for hippies, I can now admit I love hemp! Merry Hempster vegan lip balms are widely available, and a great way to keep your lips smooth and kissable. My favorite is vanilla. I've also successfully used the Merry Hempsters Tattoo Balm with Sunscreen, and I like to throw a tube in my bag when I'm unsure about the weather.

100 PERCENT VEGAN COMPANIES

Want to pick up some beauty products without having to flip over the box and read the ingredients? Here are some 100 percent vegan companies, to simplify your search for cruelty-free cosmetics.

Skin and Body

Aguacate and Co., Arbonne International, Aroma Bella, Avalon Organics, Azida Hemp Oil Products, Beauty Without Cruelty, Be Fine Food Skin Care, Bioéthique, Body Bistro, Boscia, Brown Bag Botanicals, Cactus & Ivy, Clearly Natural Soaps, Cocoon Apothecary, Coola Suncare, Desert Essence, Devita Natural Skin Care, Earthly Body, Earth Mama Angel Baby Organics, Ethically Engineered, Emerita, Everyday Organics, Exuberance, Freeman Beauty, Hugo Natural Products, Inky Loves Nature, J. R. Liggett, Keys Care, KINeSYS Sunscreen, Kirk's Natural Products, La Vie Celeste, Le FP Green Body Care, MD Skincare, Nature's Gate, Nature's Paradise, Perfect Organics, Planet Eve Organics, Obligé By Nature, Odacite, Oracle Organics, Organic Grooming by Herban Cowboy, Osea, Pharmacopeia, RARE2B Skincare, Russell Organics, Save Your World, Sevin Nyne Tanning, ShiKai, Skinvac Acne Treatment, skyn ICELAND, Strawberry Hedgehog, Théra Wise, Von Natur

Hair

ABBA Hair Care, David Babaii for Wildaid, Eco-Nature Care, Emmett Cooper Haircare, Green Body Green Planet, Hair Fix, Head Organic Hair Products, Light Mountain Natural Hair Color, Long Lovely Locks, L'uvalla, Max Green Alchemy, Original Sprout, Peter Lamas, Pureology Colour Care, RAW Hair Dye, Special Effects, Tara Smith Hair Care, The Morrocco Method, Yarok Hair

Makeup and Lip Care

Afterglow Cosmetics, Amina Cosmetics, Alexami, Cheeky Cosmetics, Cherry Crush Cosmetics, Crazy Rumors Lip Balm, Duprey Cosmetics, Earth Diva Cosmetics, Earth Goddess Minerals, Emani Minerals, Gabriel Cosmetics, Hurraw! Balm, Illuminaire Cosmetics, Lip Ink International, Musq, Obsessive Compulsive Cosmetics, Pink Quartz Minerals, Rosie Jane Cosmetics, Sevi Cosmetics, Stript Mineral Makeup, ZuZu Luxe Cosmetics

Nails

Acquarella, Anise Intense Color, Beauty Without Cruelty, Dazzle Dry, Nail-Aid, No-Miss Nail Care, Nubar, Obsessive Compulsive Cosmetics, Soulstice Spa, SpaRitual, Zoya

Leanne Mai-ly Hilgart

Business Name: Vaute Couture
Web Sites: www.VauteCouture.com; www.OnOurSleeve.com

What motivated you to start your business?

I've always been an activist and an advocate for animals, since I was in elementary school. I never could figure out what it was I wanted to do with my life; nothing fit, and nothing inspired me as much as running an animal rights group or coordinating campaigns. And then one day it hit me: Having my own business would provide an opportunity to incorporate activism into every facet of the process. I knew I had to find a challenge that would speak up for animals in an industry where they

needed a voice. I wanted to introduce innovations in fabrics that would advance cruelty-free options, showing that they are even better than conventional fabrics from animals. Animals are my drive, and fashion is my vehicle.

Do you put an emphasis on the vegan aspect of the company, and, if so, do you find that it works in your favor?

My brand of activism reaches out to a mainstream market that sees itself as kind and compassionate, shows them that vegan living is part of that self-view, and empowers them to adopt the lifestyle. Therefore, the vegan aspect is something that comes front and center, in an effort to juxtapose fashion with veganism, and educate visitors who aren't yet living vegan. For example, I named our rabbit tank top "Friends Not Test Subjects," and on the product page I feature a rescued rabbit, with the Alice Walker quotation about animals not being ours to exploit.

Having an outwardly vegan brand can have its limitations. I have to make it clear that our coats are not just for vegans, and our fabrics are in many ways superior to standard animal coat fabrics (like wool and silk). In general, it has been amazing to get to know the vegan community through this journey, and I've never felt so at home.

How do you handle any animosity toward veganism in your personal life or business?

I try to remember that everyone who's chosen to go vegan was, at one point, "pre-gan." I've heard enough stories about people who used to be so confused/angered/offended by veganism, and then later went vegan themselves, to know that everyone arrives in their own way in their own time.

What's your favorite item that you sell?

This is a toughie, but I do love our Vaute coat. It's the incarnation of why I started the line in the first place: a feminine, flirty, vegan pea coat warm enough for a Chicago winter. It has a windproof liner and an asymmetrical collar with a super full skirt. Plus, we donate all net profits of this style to the Farm Sanctuary.

Fragrance

Ambre Blends, A Perfume Organic, Bazil Essentials, Dolma, Pacifica, Tallulah Jane

While the companies listed above are 100 percent vegan, there are plenty of vegan-friendly beauty lines as well, with some having only a handful of products that are not vegan. While you'll have to check the ingredients, here are some brands to look out for that have a selection of vegan products: Alba, Bare Essentials, Beauty Without Cruelty, Dr. Bronner's, EO Products, Eyes Lips Face, Giovanni Hair Care, Hard Candy Cosmetics, Jason, John Masters Organics, Jonathan Products, Juice Beauty, Kiss My Face, LUSH, Manic Panic, Merry Hempsters, MyChelle Dermaceuticals, Origins, Suki, Tarte Cosmetics, Urban Decay Cosmetics, Weleda, and Yes to Carrots.

MINERAL MAKEUP

This craze took the world by storm a few years ago, with brands like Bare Essentials being pushed in department stores and on television. While mineral makeup is almost always vegan, one thing to consider is that it does not photograph well, especially on darker skin. Mineral makeup contains titanium dioxide, which is a white, opaque, and naturally occurring pigment. When the flash of a camera hits titanium dioxide, it can give an ashy or ghost-like tone to the skin in photographs. Have you ever seen those photos where people have tan skin and a grayish-white face? That's titanium dioxide.

Titanium dioxide is also common in sunscreen, so you may want to look out for it if you're being photographed. If you have pale skin, titanium dioxide is likely not going to be an issue, although you may look a bit shiny. Mineral makeup can be quite nice for everyday use; just keep in mind that it's not suitable for all situations.

FEMININE PRODUCTS

While there isn't often an issue with most feminine products being vegan (even though the companies that produce them may test on animals), there are other things you might want to consider. These products are going to be up close and personal with you. Do you really want pesticide-laden cotton hanging out down there? Natracare and Seventh Generation brands make organic tampons and pads, but many people are concerned with the waste from these products ending up in landfills.

Another option is a menstrual cup, like the Diva Cup or the Keeper, which collect your menstrual fluid instead of absorbing it. These cups hold more liquid than a tampon, and, if properly taken care of, can last for up to ten years, which will save you a ton of money. If you're not into the cups, Gladrags makes washable menstrual pads, as do many other sellers, while many people make their own.

For cleaning your lady parts, I Love My Muff is a vegan line of washes, sprays, and wipes, while Bikini Kitty keeps you prepped for hair removal with vegan kits for either shaving or waxing. Speaking of shaving, those little strips along most disposable razors? Not vegan! Luckily, there are some suitable brands out there; Personna, Wally, and Preserve make vegan-friendly razors, so the only thing getting hurt is you, if you nick yourself!

VEGAN SEXY TIME!

Who wants to use condoms made with milk proteins in them? I sure don't. Many of the leading brands are not suitable for vegans. Some vegan brands to look for are Glyde, Condomi, Fusion, and RFSU, and the Durex Avanti Ultima and most Pasante condoms also do not contain animal products. For lube, there are lots of water-based products on the market, and even the mainstream Astroglide is vegan.

If you're looking for other contraceptives without animal products, they can be a bit difficult to come across. For oral contraceptives, there's Femulen; Evra is a contraceptive patch, while Noristerat is an injection. If you're considering an IUD as a cheap and effective method of birth control, brands like the Mirena, Nova-T, and Paragard are worth looking into. While these contraceptives do not contain animal ingredients, they may have been tested on animals.

We don't live in a perfect society, so sometimes using medications tested on animals is unavoidable. Finding vegan contraceptives may take a bit of research, but rumor has it that vegans make better lovers, so you're going to need to be prepared!

Sometimes the easiest thing to do is hit the Internet and place an order. For a discreet source for all of your sexy needs, try TheSensualVegan.com, and for those of you who like to get a bit kinky and need some non-leather accessories to do the deed, check out VeganErotica.com.

CLEANING HOUSE

Common household products like Dawn, Gain, and Febreze are made by companies like Procter & Gamble, who test on animals; not only that—they're also filled with nasty chemicals!

Natural Cleaning Products

Go natural with all of these products, from soap to detergent and toilet paper, and check out companies like Astonish, Begley's Best, Bio Pac, BioKleen, Citra-Solv, Country Save, Cot'n Wash, Ecos, Green Forest, Marcal, Method, Mountain Green, Mrs. Meyer's, Orange-Mate, Planet, Seventh Generation, and Sun & Earth for all of your cleaning needs!

Homemade Cleaning Supplies

You can make your own supplies, ensuring they're nontoxic and saving money at the same time.

White distilled vinegar is an excellent cleaner that stops mold, cuts grease, and doesn't leave a scent behind. To make an all-purpose cleaner that's great for chrome fixtures, windows, water spots, or mirrors, add ½ cup vinegar and ¼ cup baking soda to a spray bottle, with 2 liters of water.

Baking soda is a mild abrasive and makes a great scouring product. For oven surfaces, take ¼ cup baking soda and 2 tablespoons of salt, then add enough water to make a paste; apply the paste to your surface, let it sit for five minutes, and then remove it with a damp rag.

You can also freshen your carpet and rugs by sprinkling them with baking soda; allow the baking soda to sit for at least thirty minutes, and then vacuum it up.

If your drain is clogged, try ½ cup baking soda followed by ½ cup vinegar; allow this to sit for fifteen minutes, and then follow it up with 6 cups of boiling water.

This combination can also be used to clean toilets: Allow the baking soda and vinegar to sit for a few minutes and then scrub it clean. If you have stains, use borax to scrub them off.

Polish up your furniture by combining ½ teaspoon oil (such as olive, jojoba, or mineral) with ½ cup of vinegar or lemon juice. Dip a rag in the solution and wipe down your wood surfaces.

While it may seem overwhelming at first, you can completely veganize your life; with diligence, a compassionate heart, and help from this guide, you'll be off and running in no time. If you take a false step, don't beat yourself up—it happens to all of us. Strive to do the best you can each day, and eventually it will become second nature.

Ditte

Location: Copenhagen, Denmark

Blog: Nice Things at Kajsa & Ditte's (www.nicethingsatkajsaanddittes.blogspot.com)

Favorite Dish to Cook: I guess anything brunch-related is a hit with me right now. I love serving beautiful foods, and I think it is super-fun to spend some time making the meal look mouthwatering and delicious. I have a crush on theme dinners: Indian, Italian, Japanese . . . You get the idea!

Item You Can't Live Without: I'm such a materialist! Well, besides my fiancé, I think it must be either my teeny laptop or my iPhone. Friends, recipes, shopping . . . it's all just a click away! The Internet is a huge resource, and I've met so many cool vegans online, from all over the world. Quite a few of them have spent a night or two at Ditte's Vegan Bed & Breakfast.

Funniest Vegan Moment: Oh, this leads me to think about the horrible incident of the tofu bacon. My friend and I were cooking up a dinner, which I think was mashed potatoes and tofu bacon. We were both in our own worlds, and I figured I could give the tofu bacon a little bit of sweetness, so I decided to add a teeny bit of sugar. As I turned around, my friend decided to give it a little thyme. The result was a greasy, smoky, burnt-sugar-and-thyme mess that was not edible, no matter how hard we tried to get it down. Communication is a good thing when you're in the kitchen with someone else.

The animals of the world exist for their own reasons. They were not made for humans any more than black people were made for whites or women for men.
—Alice Walker

CHAPTER 5

VEGAN FOOD

While veganism isn't only about food, the reality is that food plays a major role in our lives. From what to keep in your pantry to how to make dinner for a non-vegan, it's useful to know the basics of vegan food, so you don't end up with a house full of frozen meals and a huge grocery bill, or a nightly run to Taco Bell for a cheese-less bean burrito. Ideally, you're going to learn to cook, or at least learn how to cobble a meal together, so you can keep your intake diverse and delicious. While there are vegans out there who rely on restaurants, life does get easier, and less expensive, if you don't depend on others to feed you. Besides, you could end up with a newfound passion for cooking, which is what happened to me and many other vegans I know.

STOCKING THE VEGAN PANTRY

You don't need to lean on frozen convenience foods if you have a cupboard full of staples around at all times. By having some basics in your pantry, you should be able to whip up a meal on short notice, even if you haven't made a run for fresh fruits and vegetables. It's also useful to have a well-stocked kitchen so you're not buying massive amounts of food each week. Ideally, you should only have to buy fresh ingredients on a weekly basis while occasionally replenishing your pantry. Here are some things I like to keep on hand.

Canned Foods

Beans, the center of many meals! I have pinto, black beans, and chickpeas on hand at all times, but I also like to keep cannellini, kidney, and refried beans around.

Diced and whole tomatoes, tomato sauce, and tomato paste are always in my cupboard. Why worry about the flavor of a tomato when they're being cooked into something? Canned tomatoes are both convenient and consistent, and are even said to contain more health-boosting lycopene than fresh tomatoes!

Coconut milk for curries, soups, and chili, for the nights you just can't be bothered to cook, are other great canned goods to keep on hand.

Allison Rivers Samson

Business Name: Allison's Gourmet

Web Site / Location: www.AllisonsGourmet.com; Nevada City, California

Do you put an emphasis on the vegan aspect of the company, and, if so, do you find that it works in your favor?

Yes, we do emphasize the vegan aspect of Allison's Gourmet. Since the "V" word has become more commonplace, I think it does work in our favor to highlight that our goodies are vegan.

What's the most rewarding part of running a vegan business?

I love creating new products and testing recipes, but out of the hundred or so job titles I hold, my favorite is CTO—Chief Tasting Officer.

Do you incorporate green practices into your work?

Absolutely. We use all organic ingredients in our products, recycled and

recyclable packaging, and all of the printing paper we use is post-consumer recycled.

What's your favorite item that you sell?

Oh, that's not a fair question. It's like asking which of my children I like best. Truth be told, my favorites are our caramels, toffee, peanut butter cups, peppermint patties, brownies, and . . . well, I guess I love everything! I figure if I don't absolutely adore it, we shouldn't be selling it.

Dried Foods

Black-eyed peas, lentils, and split peas cook up quickly, so instead of going for the canned versions, I keep these dried goods on hand. Dried black beans, pinto beans, and chickpeas are certainly more cost-effective than canned, so if you're on a budget, pick these up, and then you can make a big batch to portion out and freeze.

Quinoa, rice, polenta, barley, and oats are my standbys, but couscous, millet, and bulgur are also nice to have around. It's a matter of taste, so keep the grains and seeds around that you like best.

While I have a seemingly endless assortment of different types of flour, they're hardly all crucial. I recommend all-purpose flour, whole wheat pastry flour, vital wheat gluten (the essential ingredient in seitan), and chickpea flour.

Other essential dried goods to stock are baking soda, baking powder, cornstarch, arrowroot starch, baking yeast, and cornmeal.

Nutritional yeast can be a vegan's best friend for cheesy sauces, seitan, or sprinkling on popcorn. Look for the type fortified with B12 for an extra boost, and make sure you haven't mistakenly picked up brewer's yeast, or you'll be sorry!

Noodles come in many shapes and sizes, so while I like to have soba, spaghetti, rice noodles, lasagna noodles, and brown rice penne around, you should be sure to stock all of your own favorites.

Oils, Nuts, and Seeds

Whether for sautéing, frying, or baking, having a variety of oils around comes in handy. I use a lot of olive and canola oil, but also keep peanut oil on hand for high-heat frying and Asian dishes. Coconut oil, grapeseed oil, and sesame and toasted sesame oil are great, too! Some people love flaxseed, hemp, and pumpkin-seed oil for the health benefits, although they are not recommended for cooked recipes.

Nuts are a great staple for snacking, cooking, and baking. I keep cashews, almonds, and walnuts around. Other great options are pecans, hazelnuts, and pine nuts. Peanuts (although actually legumes) are another good option.

Speaking of nuts, have some nut butters at the ready! Peanut butter and jelly sandwiches are vegan, after all. Almond butter is my spread of choice, but classic peanut butter is also a staple on toast, and sometimes I

Bahar, (bazu)

Location: Syracuse, New York

Blog: Where's the Revolution? (whereistherevolution.com)

Item You Can't Live Without: My husband, who's a better cook than me, my kitties, and my cast-iron pans.

Favorite "Accidentally Vegan" Treat: Snyder's buffalo-wing pretzel pieces

Funniest Vegan Moment: When I first went vegan, I went to my aunt's house for dinner. She had promised to cook us a vegan feast, which included some pattypan squash. Afterwards, I asked her what was in the squash. "Oh, you know, a little of this, a little of that, some butter." Silence. "What?" my aunt said. "You *need* butter to cook veggies!" We actually had a good laugh at that. There was a learning curve, but now she and most of my family members can cook a pretty mean vegan meal for me. This same aunt has since switched to soy milk—yay!

get crazy with some hazelnut or cashew butter as well. If you are allergic to nuts, try seed butters like tahini or pumpkin-seed butter. There are also nut- and seed-free spreads on the market, such as a "butter" made from peas.

Whether garnishing a dish or making a puree, some great seeds to have on hand are sesame and sunflower seeds. Pumpkin seeds are another favorite, and are especially good on salads.

Liquid smoke imparts a smoky flavor to foods when used sparingly, giving your collard greens an extra spark (without the ham hocks), and making your seitan taste like it just spent time in a smoker. It's not essential, but it's a great ingredient for flavorful food.

Refrigerated Items

Nondairy milk, Earth Balance (or other vegan margarine), tofu, tempeh, vegan mayonnaise (such as Vegenaise), soy sauce, and miso paste are essentials to have in the fridge.

Balsamic vinegar and apple cider vinegar are great for food flavoring, salad dressings, and baking. I also like to have mirin (a Japanese sweet rice wine), red and white wine vinegar, and rice wine vinegar on hand.

I also find room for jelly or jam, yellow and Dijon mustard, ketchup, hot sauces like Sriracha and Tapatio, and other condiments to keep my food well dressed.

Frozen Foods

While I tend to reserve my freezer for ice cream and leftovers, it's also a good place to store frozen peas, corn, and other vegetables of your choice, such as edamame (for a quick stir-fry add-in), or ingredients like berries (since fresh berries are not available year-round).

Ingredients for Baking

Sweetness is my weakness, so I have granulated sugar, brown sugar, and confectioners' (icing) sugar at all times. For liquid sweeteners, I stock up on maple syrup, agave nectar, brown rice syrup, and molasses.

Another baking staple is chocolate—dark, of course! A good chocolate of at least 65 percent cocoa shouldn't have milk in it, so grab some dark chocolate chips for cookies, some nice dark cocoa powder, and a chocolate bar to snack on.

Blythe Ann Boyd

Business Name: Lula's Sweet Apothecary
Web Site / Location: www.lulasweet.com; 516 East 6th Street, New York, New York

What motivated you to start your business?

After college and a brief stint in the working world, I soon discovered two important things about myself: I didn't want to work for someone else, and I wanted to work at something that was aligned with my beliefs. I became vegetarian in my teens and vegan soon thereafter, so creating a vegan business was ideal. Veganism, animal rights, and environmentalism have always been the most important causes in my life.

New York is home to so many extraordinary vegan businesses, so my partner, Derek Hackett, and I wanted to make sure we did something original. Eventually, we came up with the idea of an old-fashioned, turn-of-the-century soda fountain where we made all of the frozen desserts in-house and served up vegan versions of the classics—sundaes, splits, floats, egg creams, etcetra Lula's Sweet Apothecary was born.

Do you put an emphasis on the vegan aspect of the company, and, if so, do you find that it works in your favor?

I am open and proud about the fact that we are a vegan-owned-and-operated business. Lula's is recognized as such among the vegan community, and that, of course, works in our favor because the community spreads the word fast and is strongly supportive. Within the community, it's also reas-

suring to go into a place like Lula's and know that you can safely order anything on the menu.

Outside the community, I inadvertently learned that a lot of people still think we thrive on flavorless foods, and thus, they're put off by anything labeled "vegan." Initially, budget and time constraints limited our window signage, which would have clearly labeled the shop as "vegan," and this proved to help more than hurt the business. Many customers have come in, enjoyed their desserts, and then, upon learning they were vegan, admitted they wouldn't have come in had they known it wasn't a conventional ice cream shop. So it's a delicate balance—after all, you still have to make a living.

How do you handle any animosity toward veganism in your personal life or business?

First, I think it's important to note that I do think there's room for all forms of awareness about veganism and other causes, from the mild to the more extreme. Each style serves a purpose and is effective in its own right. In my own personal experience, I've noticed that many people are preemptively defensive, showing great animosity once they realize that I am vegan. I think there is this preconceived notion that all vegans are self-righteous and preachy, and so others are automatically reactionary. In these instances, I try to combat such notions with a milder message, so that people will let down their defenses and perhaps be more receptive to my reasons for being vegan.

There are, of course, scenarios where people are just hateful and closed-minded, and that's when anything goes. Regarding the business, I can honestly say that I've not experienced any strongly negative feedback about its vegan aspect. There are the occasional, unoriginal jokes and those who show disappointment upon learning it's a vegan establishment, but this is so rare and silly that it never really warrants a response. Most everyone, vegan and non-vegan alike, seem to be truly appreciative of our product, as well as our small-business approach.

Cassandra Jackson

Location: Chicago, Illinois

Blog: Go Vegan Go! (www.govegango.com)

Reason You Went Vegan: I had some really encouraging friends who just made veganism seem so logical, easy, and accessible. Without even pushing, they got me looking into animal rights on my own, and it just made sense once I had a better understanding of the pain and suffering my previous lifestyle was causing. I've never looked back.

Favorite Dish to Cook: I have a deep and fiery passion for macaroni and cheese, and am liable to try any vegan recipe for it that crosses my path. I've recently cracked the Soul Vegetarian recipe which is now my standby, but a basic Mac and Teese using creamy cheddar Teese is an easy favorite. Dessert-wise, I get called in to make cheesecakes. light and fluffy basic white cakes, and chocolate chip cookies on a regular basis. I'm all about the basics done on par with their non-vegan counterparts.

Favorite "Accidentally Vegan" Treat: Papa John's pizza with no cheese, extra sauce, pineapple, and banana peppers.

If you like to bake, vanilla extract is a crucial ingredient in your arsenal. Be sure to get the real deal, made from pure vanilla beans suspended in alcohol, and not imitation vanilla, which is a synthetic product. Vanilla is the second-most-expensive spice in the world, next to saffron, and is typically used to flavor desserts and intensify chocolate flavors. I like Nielsen-Massey Madagascar Bourbon Vanilla, but I have also made my own extract from vanilla beans, with great success. Many avid bakers also keep lemon, orange, and almond extract around, and I like to include chocolate, coconut, mint, coffee, strawberry, and maple for extra exciting desserts!

HOMEMADE VANILLA EXTRACT

It's easier than you think to make your own vanilla extract. All you need is some vanilla beans, a bottle of vodka, and patience. Vanilla beans can be pricey in stores, but there are great shops online, like Vanilla Products USA, that sell them for much less.

10 to 12 vanilla beans (B grade are ideal)

750 ml of decent-quality vodka, 75 to 80 proof

Cut the vanilla beans lengthwise with a knife to within ¼ to ½ inch of the end, leaving the split bean intact at the bottom. Pour a small amount of vodka out of the bottle; then, add the split beans and reseal the bottle. Shake the bottle, and then place it in a dark area, like a cupboard, for at least eight to twelve weeks, shaking occasionally. After eight to twelve weeks, you should have deep, amber-colored extract. Not only can you use the extract, but you can also keep adding vodka to the bottle to keep

the extract replenished. To keep your extract going, add new vanilla beans from time to time, although it's not necessary within the first year. Some people have had the same extract for ten years!

SPICES

No great chef is without an extensive collection of spices! It is crucial that you have a wide selection of spices for truly flavorful food, or you'll fall prey to the "Vegan food is bland" myth. Ideally, you'll be able to buy locally in bulk, so you can have a little or a lot based on usage, and keep everything fresh. If you can't find a good local source, take to the Internet and order from Penzey's, Frontier, or other fine spice retailers. While your local grocer will have spices in jars, it's hard to know how fresh these are, and they tend to be less potent. I like Indian or Asian grocers for inexpensive and specialty spices, and I've found that excess spices can be frozen in airtight containers, with no ill effects. Investing in some airtight spice containers is worthwhile, as they will keep your spices fresh while reducing the amount of wasted packaging.

Here's what I recommend, starting with the most crucial herbs and spices and then moving on to what you should add as soon as possible. Start with basil, black pepper, cayenne, mild chile powder (not the much spicier blends of dried chili powders), cinnamon, coriander, cumin, curry powder, oregano, rosemary, sea salt, and thyme.

As your spice rack grows, along with your cooking prowess, add allspice, whole bay leaves, caraway seeds, cardamom, cloves, cumin seeds, dill, fennel seeds, garam masala, garlic powder, ginger, mustard seeds, marjoram, nutmeg, onion powder, paprika (Hungarian and smoked), parsley, poppy seeds, red pepper flakes, sage, sesame seeds, and tarragon.

You'll find there are many more seasonings out there, including asafetida, saffron, and sumac, so don't be afraid to pick some up and experiment!

KITCHEN TOOLS

If you're going to start cooking, you're not going to get very far without the proper equipment. While we can't all be outfitted with All-Clad cookware and Wusthof knives, there are plenty of mid-range products that are going to last a lot longer than a $2 IKEA knife. I recommend you start within your budget, try secondhand shops for great-quality finds, and then slowly upgrade your tools as you are able.

Now, here are some basics to get cookin'!

Secret Supper

Business Name: Secret Supper

Web Site: www.vegansecretsupper.com

Do you put an emphasis on the vegan aspect of the company, and, if so, do you find that it works in your favor?

Secret Supper's approach is quite subtle. I wanted it to be nonthreatening for a non-vegan to come to, and wanted the food to speak for itself as delicious food, and not just delicious **vegan** *food.*

Are the people who attend your events typically vegan?

I would say a little less than half. Sometimes it will be a group with one vegan or vegetarian, and the rest are full-on meat eaters.

Do you find you can change people's minds about veganism through food?

The non-vegans who come definitely leave with their views on vegan food expanded in a positive way. I also don't really cook with much soy or tofu, which can be threatening to non-vegans, though I am always aware of making a well-rounded supper, nutrition-wise.

What is your favorite menu item you've made?

My sweet potato coconut crème brulée and cheesecake have been everyone's favorite, but I think my personal favorite would have to be my lentil walnut tortière.

What advice do you have for people who want to engage in "culinary activism" and spread the word about veganism through food?

Let the food speak for itself. Pushing facts and animal rights comments can get meat eaters and the like very defensive. People just need to know they can still have amazing food without meat and dairy.

Sample Menu

- Butternut apple puree with chipotle apple reduction and coconut sour cream
- Roasted beet and apple spring rolls with hazelnuts, avocado mustard, and greens with lemon soy rosemary vinaigrette
- Portobello tortellini with raw sage cashew cheese
- White chocolate brownie cheesecake with coconut peanut butter ice cream

A quality chef's knife can do it all! My 9-inch Shun chef's knife is my right-hand man in the kitchen, and once you find your perfect knife, you'll wonder how you ever lived without it. Other useful knives are serrated bread knives and small paring knives.

Leave that plate alone and get yourself a cutting board! I like a sturdy bamboo board, so it doesn't slip when you use it.

Hand tools make life easier, so I like to have a wooden spoon, slotted spoon, a flat spatula, a silicone spatula, and a pasta spoon at the ready. Other small tools I frequently use are measuring spoons and cups, a grater, a microplane zester, and a vegetable peeler.

Of course, you need bowls for mixing and serving. Get yourself a set of various sizes in stainless steel or glass.

You cannot cook without pots and pans! The ones I use most often are a 12-inch sauté pan, a small saucepan, a large saucepan, and a large stockpot, all with lids. I prefer stainless steel, but cast iron is a great option as well. Nonstick pans can be useful, but due to the issues associated with scraping the bottom and the toxins that can be emitted, I personally skip them.

I can't even begin to get into all the baking accoutrements I have, so I'll leave you with the basics. I recommend a large baking sheet, somewhere around 11 x 17, a glass casserole dish, 9-inch cake pans, a standard-size cupcake/muffin tin, a loaf pan, and a cooling rack. I also love jumbo muffin pans, mini muffin pans, and Bundt pans, but this is coming from someone who has a pan to make a foot-tall cupcake, so decide what you need and go with it!

Speaking of baking, an oven thermometer is a must! Chances are your oven temperature is a bit off, which means your baking results will be off when following recipes. Revolutionize your kitchen with an oven thermometer. Nothing fancy is required, but they are invaluable in any kitchen.

While a food processor isn't 100 percent necessary, you're going to be skipping a fair amount of recipes without one. They also have attachments to chop and shred vegetables, so they easily earn their keep.

Some optional but fun items include an oil spray bottle (the glass ones are best), a salad spinner, a garlic press, a citrus squeezer, a bamboo steamer, an immersion blender, and a Silpat nonstick baking mat. I use all of these things often, so I suggest you get them if your budget allows. You don't have to buy them all in one go, so enjoy building up your kitchen gradually.

WHAT VEGANS EAT

Okay, you have a bunch of delicious ingredients in your pantry; now what? When meal-time comes, you may wonder what other vegans eat. While making vegan versions of your favorite dishes is a great option, it's also nice to expand your horizons and try new cuisines and ingredients. Next time someone asks you what the hell vegans eat, show them this list of ideas, or just use it to inspire your own creations.

Breakfast

Oatmeal with almond butter, dried fruit, and/or chopped nuts; pancakes or waffles; nondairy yogurt topped with granola; tofu scramble with a side of tempeh bacon; biscuits with vegan gravy; English muffins topped with peanut butter and jelly; a green smoothie; a bagel with Tofutti cream cheese; Two-Bean Confetti Hash (recipe on page 139); a breakfast burrito; a whole wheat or bran muffin.

Lunch

Hummus wrap with fresh vegetables; green salad with chickpeas, beans, and other vegetable toppings; tofu salad sandwich; quinoa salad with beans and vegeta-bles; chickpea salad sandwich; bean, macaroni, or potato salad; veggie burger; peanut butter and jelly sandwich; falafel in pita or lavash bread.

Dinner

Beans and greens over a grain; spaghetti in marinara sauce; bean tacos or burritos; baked tofu, rice, and steamed vegetables; lentil vegetable curry; baked beans and tofu pups; stir-fry with pan-fried tofu; soup, stew, or chili; Moroccan Chickpea and Kale Tagine with Quinoa (recipe on page 168); barbecue seitan sandwiches with coleslaw; Sloppy Joes (recipe on page 174).

RECIPES

If you don't have much (or any!) experience with cooking, figuring out how to feed yourself can be overwhelming. Luckily, there are endless recipe resources both in print and online. While it's impossible to name them all, here are a few of my favorites:

Veganomicon and *Vegan Cupcakes Take Over the World* by Isa Chandra Moskowitz and Terry Hope Romero

Vegan Brunch and *Vegan with a Vengeance* by Isa Chandra Moskowitz

Viva Vegan! by Terry Hope Romero

My Sweet Vegan by Hannah Kaminsky

The Joy of Vegan Baking by Colleen Patrick-Goudreau

500 Vegan Recipes by Celine Steen and Joni Marie Newman

Everyday Dish (www.everydaydish.tv)

Fat-Free Vegan Kitchen (www.fatfreevegan.com)

Bittersweet Blog (www.bittersweetblog.com)

Have Cake, Will Travel (www.havecakewilltravel.com)

Seitan Is My Motor (www.seitanismymotor.com)

The Messy Vegetarian Cook (www.messyvegetariancook.com)

Manjula's Kitchen (www.manjulaskitchen.com)

VegWeb.com has thousands of great recipes; just make sure to read the ratings!

VegNews is a vegan magazine with many recipes among the articles, and their Web site (VegNews.com) contains a large amount of recipes, as well.

MILK WITHOUT THE MOO AND OTHER DAIRY SUBSTITUTES

Dairy products are by far the easiest thing to substitute, as there are plenty of nondairy counterparts. Soy, rice, almond, hemp, oat, and more can be made into milk, yogurt, cheese, ice cream, cream cheese, and even heavy cream. One thing to be aware of is that the taste of nondairy products varies greatly from brand to brand, so if you don't enjoy soy milk right away, try another brand, or a different type of nondairy milk. Another thing to consider is that different milks will suit different needs. You may like sweetened vanilla almond milk for your cereal, but unsweetened soy milk for cooking. Some of my personal favorites are Tempt Vanilla Hemp Milk for cereal and cookie dunking, Almond Breeze Unsweetened Almond Milk for cooking and baking, So Delicious Coconut Milk yogurt for eating, Wildwood Plain Soy Yogurt for baking and savory sauces, Cheezly soy cheese, Earth Balance vegan margarine, and both Temptation and Tempt ice cream. There's a whole world of nondairy products out there, and with a bit of research and taste testing, you'll discover what suits you best.

EGG REPLACING MADE EASY

Eggs can have different functions in a recipe, from leavening to moisture content. The trick to replacing eggs in a recipe is to see what role they play and then proceed with your recipe. In cases where a recipe contains more than two eggs, or in a recipe where the primary structure comes from eggs, I recommend looking for an already-vegan recipe in a cookbook or online, unless you're an experienced vegan baker who is not afraid of a few failures.

Some options for egg replacers are silken tofu, cornstarch or arrowroot powder, soy yogurt, and mashed banana. There are also commercially available powdered egg replacers such as Ener-G that work well in certain instances (i.e., in some baked goods). Many times the eggs can be left out entirely while the baking soda or powder and amount of liquid can be adjusted accordingly. You may notice that many vegan recipes don't have a specific egg replacer in them at all. Experiment to find what works best for you, but once you get the hang of it, it's a breeze!

Options to Replace One Egg

- ¼ cup blended silken tofu works well for denser items, such as brownies or Bundt cakes, and of course, it's good for savory applications as well.
- ¼ cup soy yogurt is great for moist muffins, cakes, and quick breads.
- 1 tablespoon flaxseeds, ground, or 2 ½ teaspoons pre-ground flax added to 3 tablespoons water and blended is a good binder for cookies, pancakes, and whole-grain items. Flax has a nutty, earthy taste to it and tends to make things bake on the crisper side, so it may not be best for cakes and other delicately flavored goods.
- ¼ cup mashed banana or applesauce is a good option for moisture in muffins and quick breads, but they don't aid in leavening, so make sure you have enough baking soda or powder in the batter.
- 2 tablespoons cornstarch, arrowroot, or potato starch is another option that works to bind items together in both savory and sweet dishes.

CONVERTING NON-VEGAN RECIPES

Sometimes you're dying to make your grandma's famous snickerdoodle cookies or the holiday lasagna of your youth; instead of going without, "veganize" it! With alternate milks, cheese substitutes, mock meats, and egg replacers, vegan products have made leaps and bounds, and that makes veganizing recipes easier than ever. Making cookies? Try a flax egg. Need ricotta? Try making it with tofu and some seasonings. Looking for melty cheese? Vegan brands like Teese, Daiya, Cheezly, and Follow Your Heart have it handled.

While milk substitutes are the easiest out there, with soy, almond, rice, hemp, oat, and others readily available, there are some trickier cases, like egg whites. Looking to make an angel food cake? When you figure it out, please share! Recipes with more than four eggs may seem a bit difficult to veganize, but the great news is, there's likely a recipe out there for something similar already. It won't be the classic family recipe, but who knows? You may start a new tradition!

HIDDEN ANIMAL INGREDIENTS: WHAT TO WATCH OUT FOR!

Casein, whey, albumen, vitamin D3, carmine, confectioners' glaze, and more! It seems like every day a new item is found to be from an animal source, or recipes are changed on previously vegan items. It's enough to make you go crazy, but don't, because veganism isn't about feeling deprived or being driven mad. A great resource is *Animal Ingredients A–Z* by the E. G. Smith Collective, a very thorough book that lists all of the ingredients you can think of, including items which may or may not be sourced from animals. Of course, you don't need to consult a lengthy tome to learn about animal ingredients; the Internet is also a great resource. Check out the guide at Veganwolf. com, or get your Google on.

THAT'S NOT VEGAN?!

Sometimes it's a shock to find out that something is not vegan, and with animal ingredients often hidden behind indistinguishable names, it's no wonder vegans slip up from time to time. Here are some items that imply they are vegan, or would naturally be considered vegan, but are not. Buyer beware!

Nondairy Creamer

A staple in many offices, and possibly the silliest thing on this list, nondairy creamer typically contains sodium caseinate, a milk protein, meaning it's not nondairy at all!

Some Soy/Rice Cheeses

While several brands are safe for vegans, look for casein (a milk protein) in some varieties, such as Soya Kaas, which they claim help it melt and stretch. With brands like Daiya and Teese melting perfectly, who needs casein?

Noah's Bagels

Flour, water, salt—what else does a bagel need? According to the bagel chain, Noah's, they need the dough conditioner L-cysteine, which can be either human hair, or, in the case of these bagels, duck feathers! Not only is it not vegan-friendly, but it's also downright disgusting!

Fortified Cereals

You would think that a cereal fortified with vitamins would be a good thing—that is, unless the cereal contains animal-derived vitamins such as vitamin D3. While vitamin D1 and D2 are vegan, vitamin D3—also known as cholecalciferol—is typically sourced from lanolin (sheep's wool) or fish, and commonly found in cereals made by General Mills and other large manufacturers.

Planters Peanuts

Yes, really. While these legumes are a great staple in a vegan diet, for some unknown reason Planters peanuts contain gelatin.

Other Items

Other items to watch out for include confectioners' glaze in sprinkles and other candy, milk ingredients in dark chocolate, beef tallow in McDonald's french fries in the United States, eggs in meat substitutes like Quorn and Morningstar Farms, gelatin in Altoids mints, and eggs, milk, honey, or whey in some hot dog and burger buns.

Sugar Isn't Vegan?!

You'll likely run across some people who assume that vegans can't eat sugar, and that all of your baked goods are magically sugar-free. How this myth evolved, I don't know, but one reason may be that some sugar is not technically vegan. Cane sugar accounts for about half the sugar in the United States, and can be refined with animal-bone charcoal to remove impurities and whiten the color. The bone charcoal is likely not found in the final product—it's even certified "kosher pareve"—but the bones of animals are used in the processing of about half the cane sugar in the United States, so it is up to you to decide how you feel about this, and what you want to avoid.

The other half of the sugar in the United States, and much of the world, is beet sugar, which does not use animal ingredients in the processing, so it's completely safe for vegans. All organic sugar, whether cane or beet, is suitable for vegans, as well as other sugar types like turbinado, sugar in the raw, Sucanat, fructose, date sugar, and liquid sugars like agave nectar, maple syrup, corn syrup, molasses, brown rice syrup, and barley malt syrup. Don't worry—you're not going to come up short on ways to sweeten your treats!

Alyssa

Location: New York City

Blog: Alyssa in a Coma (alyssainacoma.blogspot.com)

Favorite Dish to Cook: Fancy birthday cakes for my pals! I always have a ball sneakily finding out their favorite flavors and then surprising them with beautiful confections that just happen to be vegan. The more obnoxious, the better. Aren't birthdays the best?!

Item You Can't Live Without: Sundaes from Lula's Sweet Apothecary in Manhattan. I like to pretend as much as possible that it is the year 1958, so this place helps me live that dream on a daily basis. They also make the best ice cream there ever was, and it's all vegan. My usual sundae consists of peanut butter and jelly ice cream with marshmallow sauce, rainbow sprinkles, and, of course, whipped cream and a cherry on top!

Favorite Vegan Hater Comeback: "Eggs equal chicken periods."

JUNK FOOD

Sure, there are vegans who prefer healthy foods, but for those who like to indulge themselves from time to time, there's a world of vegan junk food in your local supermarket! I can't condone any of the companies behind these products, but do your research and decide what works for you. These are just a few of the "accidentally vegan" treats out there, but be sure to check the ingredients, as they are prone to changing when you least expect it.

Oreo cookies (United States and Canada), Nutter Butter, Chick-O-Stick, Fritos, Red Vines, Airheads, Blow Pops, Cracker Jack, Peanut Chews, Laffy Taffy, Lemonheads, Mambas, Teddy Grahams, Skittles (USA), Sour Patch Kids, Swedish Fish, Twizzlers, Reese's Shell Topping, Spicy Sweet Chili Doritos, Bac-Os, and Smucker's Marshmallow Topping.

FIVE THINGS NOT TO FEED A NON-VEGAN

Even the best chef can scare an omnivore away from vegan food by feeding them items from uncharted territory. While your friends and family may warm up eventually, and plenty of people are receptive to a plant-based diet, here are some items you may not want to use when first introducing people to vegan cuisine:

1) **Tofu**

The punch line to many vegetarian jokes, tofu has a bad reputation in the meat-eaters' world. A white block of goo to the untrained eye, most people are reluctant to try tofu unless it's hidden deep in their Pad Thai. We know it's great when seasoned correctly, but give yourself a break and save the tofu for another time, or just hide the silken variety in the dessert!

2) **Mock Meats**

People love to ask, "Why are vegetarians always eating meat substitutes? Why not just eat the real thing?" The issue with serving "veggie chicken" is that it's going to be compared with the fleshy version it's trying to emulate. It will not be the same, and therefore will likely be deemed inferior, animal-cruelty issues aside. Avoid the questions and comparisons by sticking with foods that aren't masquerading as something else, until you know that your friends and family are open to vegan meats.

3) **Nondairy Cheese**

Realistically, vegan cheese is not the same as dairy cheese. First of all, vegan cheese doesn't contain the opiate-like casein, so we're not all addicted to it, but it's also not made exactly the same way. Vegan cheeses have made some serious progress, but they're certainly not something you want to be serving up to the "But I could never give up cheese!" crowd.

4) Soy Milk

As an ingredient in a recipe, sure, but in a glass by their dinner plate? No way! Think about the first time you tried soy milk; there's a chance you liked it, but more than likely you found it a bit weird, or weren't quite sure what to think. Don't inflict that on your dining companion!

5) Nutritional Yeast

"Nooch" is great for folding into a tofu scramble, sprinkling on popcorn, or making a cheesy-style sauce, but the mere mention of "yeast" being put in someone's food can send them running. Nutritional yeast is not for everyone—even some vegans dislike it—so skip the "Mac and Yeast" for your inaugural vegan feast and stick to more-familiar dishes.

FIVE THINGS TO FEED A NON-VEGAN

So, you want to impress friends or family with vegan cuisine? While I started you off with what *not* to serve, I couldn't forget to equip you with what does tend to go over well with all crowds. Here are some dishes that will ensure they won't miss the meat! The key here is not to serve them "vegan food," but to serve them familiar dishes that just happen to be vegan!

1) Chili

Vegetarian chili is so common, your local grocery store likely has a canned version. Of course, you can whip up your own version with beans, lentils, sweet potato cubes, and various other vegetables. Chili is so easy to make, you likely have a fair amount of the ingredients in your pantry right now. Check out the Basic Three-Bean Chili recipe on page 154 as a starting point for your chili creations.

2) Soup

There are so many types of soup out there, from bean to split pea, noodle to vegetable, and a plethora of options in between. Everyone eats soup, whether it's hearty, light, cold, or hot. Go wild! Make an extra-special meal out of it by serving your soup in a sourdough bread bowl with a salad on the side.

3) Potatoes

French fries, Tater Tots, mashed potatoes and gravy, and baked potatoes are all familiar comfort foods that are easily made vegan. In cases where dairy items may be used (like butter or sour cream), try the vegan counterparts, like Earth Balance and Tofutti Sour Supreme. (By the way, despite being full of crap, Bac-Os are completely vegan, so don't be afraid to dress up that baked potato.) At the Baked Potato Shop in Edinburgh, Scotland, they have everything from chili and curried corn salad to hummus and even vegan haggis to put in potatoes. Get creative with the toppings, and no one will think anything is missing.

4) Viva Italiano!

Despite the cheese, Italian fare can be easy to serve to anyone. Start your guests off with a salad topped with vinaigrette and a bowl of minestrone soup; then move on to garlic bread and a massive plate of spaghetti in marinara sauce. Classic and delicious, not to mention something non-vegans eat all the time.

5) Mexican Fiesta!

Fill up those tortillas and taco shells with refried beans, rice, salsa, guacamole, and fresh vegetables like onion, lettuce, and tomato. I like to set up a make-your-own taco station for my family at get-togethers, and with enough options on the table, no one will notice the absence of animal products. If you feel the need, you can find Tofutti Sour Supreme at many grocery stores, or you can make a cashew cream (see the recipe for Lemon Cream Sauce on page 159 for a twist on cashew cream). Just save the soy-cheese quesadillas for another time!

TOFU TIPS

The first time I used tofu in my own kitchen I was a teenage vegetarian, and it was a watery mess crumbled throughout a stir-fry. I couldn't understand why it didn't look or taste anything like the beloved little cubes of deliciousness at my local Chinese restaurant, and I swore off tofu for quite some time. Fast-forward to my mid-twenties, when I really started to learn how to cook, and I figured out that not all tofu is created equal. Those vacuum-packed tofu blocks? Not typically meant for stir-fry! Tofu comes in silken, soft, medium, firm, and extra-firm, with each variation having its place.

Silken is very soft and smooth—a great option for desserts like chocolate silk pie, which is often the first dessert a vegan makes on their own. The most commonly used tofu for grilling and pan-frying is *firm* or *extra-firm*.

Also, pressing the moisture out is where it's at! Want lots of flavor in your tofu? Take some of the moisture out! The age-old trick is to wrap your block of tofu in a cloth and then place heavy books on top of it, for anywhere from thirty minutes to overnight. After the moisture is out, cut your tofu up and slip it into a marinade for maximum flavor before grilling, frying, or baking.

Some people like to freeze their tofu to make it extra chewy and spongy, and while it's not my first choice, you may find you love it! My favorite tofu is by Hodo Soy Beanery, a smooth and amazingly fresh tofu without preservatives available in the San Francisco Bay Area. Look for something similar in your neighborhood at farmers' markets, Asian markets, and in the bulk sections at your local natural foods co-op. The texture is unlike any other!

Omnivores don't eat unseasoned flesh, so why would you eat unseasoned tofu? Tofu is a fabulous blank canvas for your favorite flavors, and can be marinated in something as simple as your favorite barbecue sauce. Asian-inspired marinades, Italian seasoning, dry rubs—just about anything fits with this delicious protein. For great recipes like the perfect tofu scramble, check out *Veganomicon* by Isa Chandra Moskowitz and Terry Hope Romero.

ATTENTION, TEMPEH HATERS!

A lot of vegans have started out with distaste for the block of fermented soybeans known as tempeh. It can be bitter or bland if not handled well, but in the right hands, it can be succulent and flavorful. Want to get the most out of your tempeh? First of all, steam or braise the funk out! Ten to fifteen minutes in a steamer or in a simmering pan of water, and you can kiss that bitterness good-bye and get to marinating. Tempeh doesn't absorb marinades like tofu does, so the best option is a sauce that's going to glaze the outside. Great tempeh should be chewy with a slight nuttiness to it, which makes for a great meat replacement in sandwiches, salads, stews, and on the grill.

If you are hesitant about trying tempeh for the first time, try the Sloppy Joes recipe on page 174, using the tempeh variation. The sauce is thick and tangy, and the tempeh is crumbled throughout so it's more about texture than anything else. Not all brands of tempeh are equal, so don't be afraid to try other brands before you swear off tempeh. Personally, I'm a fan of the tempeh by Turtle Island.

WHEAT MEAT IS FOR LOVERS!

Seitan is a delicious meat analog made from wheat gluten, and it's the basis of many veganized favorites, including the Chicago Diner's Radical Reuben and homemade Chicken Wingz. While it may seem difficult to make seitan, it's actually quite simple,

Jess

Location: Portland, Oregon

Blog / Web Site: Get Sconed (getsconedpdx.com) and Stumptown Vegans (stumptownvegans.com)

Reason You Went Vegan: I became a vegetarian at age ten, due to my picky nature and the fact that I didn't enjoy most meats because I connected them with animals. At nineteen, I took a class on animal philosophy in college and learned more about veganism. That led me to discover what I considered to be natural for my human body. I realized organic/cage-free dairy and eggs were ridiculous, and contrary to my vegetarianism, so I went vegan.

Favorite Dish to Cook: Italian-influenced stuffed mushrooms with toasted nuts, garlic, red wine, spices, and more—awesome! They'd make my mom proud.

Favorite "Accidentally Vegan" Treat: The every-couple-of-years, movie-theater popcorn, in all its horrifying, napkins-necessary glory.

as it typically contains vital wheat gluten, liquid, and an assortment of spices. Seitan can be braised, simmered, steamed, or baked. When using the simmered method, the seitan can develop a "brainy" texture if the heat is too high. I find the steaming method, a wondrous discovery by *Everyday Dish TV* guru Julie Hasson, to be the easiest and the best way to try different flavor combinations. Baked seitan is another foolproof way to create wheat-meat goodness without the worries of overcooking it. For a simmered version, check out page 170 for Jenn Shagrin's Cracked Coriander Seed and Chai Tea–Rubbed Vegan Steak Lo Mein.

VEGAN ON THE CHEAP

We can't all afford to have a pantry full of organic produce from Whole Foods, or to dine out every night, so for those of us who can't, here are some tricks to keep your grocery bill down.

Bulk Bins

If you have a local spot where you can buy dry goods in bulk, you can save a lot of money. Beans, grains, pasta, oats, flour, and even things like chocolate and nutritional yeast can be found in bulk departments. Not only is the price lower when you buy in bulk, but you can also buy smaller amounts when you have less cash to spend. If you don't have bulk bins, a bag of dried beans is still going to be cheaper than a can, just like a bag of rice will be cheaper than precooked bagged rice. Feel like dried beans are too time-consuming? An Internet search for "90-minute no-soak beans" will help you bypass hours of bean preparation, and keep you well stocked for less money.

Fresh Produce

Fruits and vegetables are a staple of a vegan diet, and while this can be pricey, it doesn't have to be. Local, seasonal produce tends to be cheaper, especially at farmers' markets, and it's also better for the environment. Hearty and inexpensive staples like potatoes, cabbage, and onions can get you through skint weeks. A good rule of thumb: If it's under $1 a pound, you can buy as much as you want or need; $1 to $2 a pound is still affordable, but should be considered carefully; and items that cost over $2 a pound are on the pricey side, and should be bought in small quantities.

When you find great sales on produce, consider purchasing large amounts of it to cook larger meals that you can then portion out and freeze for later consumption. The benefit of this is when you don't have enough in the pantry to whip something up, or you're tired of the same cabbage and potatoes, you'll have an alternate option waiting for you, without all the time it takes to prepare a fresh meal. It can also be a way to enjoy produce that has gone out of season.

While it's ideal to buy organic fruits and vegetables, it's not an option for everyone. The "Dirty Dozen" is a list of produce from the Environmental Working Group that has been deemed most likely to contain pesticides, so you should always try to go organic when you purchase them.

The Dirty Dozen

1) Celery
2) Peaches
3) Strawberries
4) Apples
5) Blueberries
6) Nectarines
7) Bell Peppers
8) Spinach
9) Kale
10) Cherries
11) Potatoes
12) Grapes (imported)

On the other hand, the following "Clean Fifteen," also from the Environmental Working Group, lists those fruits and vegetables that are least likely to contain pesticide residue, so if you can't afford the organic version, you can opt for conventionally grown.

The Clean Fifteen

1) Onion
2) Avocado
3) Sweet corn
4) Pineapple
5) Mango
6) Peas
7) Asparagus
8) Kiwi
9) Cabbage
10) Eggplant
11) Cantaloupe
12) Watermelon
13) Grapefruit
14) Sweet Potato
15) Honeydew Melon

The world of vegan food is diverse and plentiful, and hopefully you'll take the time to explore it. I've tried so many new foods, truly learned how to cook, and started to really appreciate the food I fuel my body with, and I hope you will do the same! It's refreshing to care about what you eat, not to mention rewarding, as you get to enjoy delicious cuisine from all around the world. While you may feel overwhelmed at first, take it slow, eat within your comfort zone, and then begin to explore new foods. Who knows? You could be the next vegan cookbook author or food-blog guru!

Our task must be to free ourselves . . .
by widening our circle of compassion
to embrace all living creatures and the
whole of nature and its beauty.
—Albert Einstein

CHAPTER 6

GET STARTED IN THE KITCHEN: RECIPES

Whether you've never picked up a pan or you're already a seasoned chef, you can tackle these recipes. From savory to sweet, there's something for everyone here, including plenty of dishes you can serve to a broad audience, vegan and non-vegan alike. I've tried to keep it fun and flavorful, and I've kept an eye on the clock, as many of the dishes can be prepared in thirty minutes or less. Don't be afraid to change things to suit your tastes or the contents of your pantry; experimenting in the kitchen can produce delicious results.

Most of all, have fun! Being vegan isn't about eating plain tofu and wilted sprouts; it's about compassion and a cruelty-free diet, which doesn't have to taste bland or uninspired. Now, grab your knives and get ready for a culinary adventure!

BRUNCH

TWO-BEAN CONFETTI HASH

Serves 4 to 6 as an entree, 8 as a side.

Sometimes you need a change from the typical tofu scramble. Along comes this delicious bean hash to save the day! Simple, quick, and tasty, this hash is a great way to get started in the morning.

  2 tablespoons olive oil

  1 medium onion, diced

  1 medium carrot, cut in ¼-inch pieces

  1 pound of potatoes, cut in ¼-inch pieces

  3 to 4 cloves of garlic, minced

  1 bell pepper, green or red, diced

1 ½ teaspoons thyme

½ teaspoon tarragon

salt and pepper, to taste

1 (15-ounce) can of black beans, drained and rinsed

1 (15-ounce) can of kidney beans, drained and rinsed

A handful of spinach (optional)

Preheat a large skillet with oil over medium heat; add the onion, potatoes, and carrot. Cover and cook about for 10 to 12 minutes, stirring often, until the potatoes soften and onions are translucent. Add the garlic, bell pepper, thyme,

Photo Credit: Nicole Carpenter

tarragon, and a pinch of salt and pepper; stir. Cook until everything has softened and the potatoes are lightly browned (about 5 minutes). Mix in the beans and spinach (if using), and cook until heated through and the spinach is wilted (3 to 5 minutes). Remove from heat, taste for seasoning, and serve with ketchup, Tabasco, or your favorite breakfast condiment.

CORNMEAL-CRUST SHIITAKE MUSHROOM AND CORN QUICHE

Serves 4 to 6.

Not just for breakfast, this is a quick and delicious meal in a pan, with no eggs required! Ideally, you'll use a food processor for the crust and the filling, but if you don't have one, you can still make this with a fork and some muscle. Quiche is best served when it has cooled for at least 20 minutes, so feel free to make this in advance and serve it at room temperature. This tastes even better the next day!

Crust:

1 cup all-purpose flour

¼ cup cornmeal

½ teaspoon salt

¼ cup (approx. 2 ounces) cold Earth Balance or other vegan margarine, cut into pieces

3 tablespoons ice water

Filling:

- ½ pound shiitake mushrooms, de-stemmed and sliced in thin strips, about ⅛ inch
- 2 tablespoons soy sauce
- 2 tablespoons olive oil
- ½ teaspoon salt
- ¼ teaspoon liquid smoke (optional)
- 1 small onion, finely diced
- 1 small red bell pepper, diced
- 2 cups corn, fresh or frozen (and thawed)
- 14 to 16 ounces firm tofu
- 2 tablespoons lemon juice
- 2 tablespoons tahini
- 1 teaspoon thyme
- ½ teaspoon turmeric
- ½ teaspoon salt
- Pepper, to taste

Photo Credit: Hannah Kaminsky

Preheat the oven to 350°F, and then make the crust so it can chill while you prepare the rest of the quiche. Place the flour, cornmeal, and salt in a food processor and pulse to combine. Add the cold margarine and pulse until pea-size clusters have formed. With the food processor on, add the ice water in a solid stream. As soon as dough forms, stop the processor (a few chunks are okay). Place the dough in plastic wrap, flatten it into a disc, and place it in the freezer. This can also be made a day in advance and stored overnight in the refrigerator.

Heat a deep skillet over medium-high heat. Add the mushrooms, stirring them until they start to release liquid. Add the soy sauce, 1 tablespoon of oil, salt, and liquid smoke, and stir to combine. Cook over high heat, stirring often, until the liquid is absorbed and the mushrooms start to dry out and get crisp (about 10 minutes). If the mushrooms stick, do not add water; just scrape the bits from the bottom and keep stirring. Once the liquid has absorbed, place the mushrooms on a piece of paper towel and set aside.

Place the skillet back on the stove over medium heat and add the rest of the oil. Sauté the onion and bell pepper, about 5 to 7 minutes, until the onion is translucent. Add the corn and cook until heated through and tender, 5 to 7 minutes for fresh, 3 to 5 minutes for frozen. Remove from heat and set aside.

Rinse out the food processor and crumble the tofu into it. Pulse the tofu until it is broken up and there are no large chunks left. Add the lemon juice, tahini, thyme, turmeric, and salt and pepper, and puree until smooth. Pour the tofu mixture into a mixing bowl, and then fold in the corn mixture and the sautéed mushrooms.

Remove the crust from the freezer and roll it out to fit a 9-inch pie or tart pan. Press the crust into the pan, making sure the edges are even. Add the tofu mixture, pressing to pack everything in. You may have some excess filling, depending on your tofu. Bake for 35 to 40 minutes, until the top looks dry and the middle is firm. Remove from the oven and allow to cool for at least 20 minutes, and then serve.

SIMPLE FLUFFY BISCUITS AND WHITE COUNTRY GRAVY
BY CHRIS AND CRYSTAL TATE

Yields 9 to 10 biscuits.

Vegan biscuits and gravy are a craze sweeping the nation in greasy spoons all over America! Actually, they're a longtime staple of Southern dining and the rest of us are finally catching up. Chris and Crystal Tate, the famous duo behind the company Food for Lovers Queso, are born-and-raised Texans who know their way around a biscuit and some gravy. These biscuits are insanely simple, and delicious when smothered in a peppery white gravy. Whether enjoying them for brunch or for dinner, they're downright delicious anytime!

Biscuits:

Photo Credit: Nicole Carpenter

2 cups flour

1 tablespoon baking powder

½ teaspoon baking soda

¾ teaspoon salt

⅓ cup shortening

1 cup vegan buttermilk, chilled (1 cup soy milk plus 1 teaspoon apple cider vinegar)

Preheat the oven to 325°F. In a large mixing bowl, use a whisk to combine flour, baking powder, baking soda, and salt.

In a small bowl, make your buttermilk by combining 1 cup (chilled) soy milk and 1 teaspoon apple cider vinegar. Set aside for 3 minutes.

Drop the shortening into the large mixing bowl. Using your fingers, pinch the shortening into the dry ingredients until you have a coarse mixture. Make a well in the center of the coarse mixture. Pour in chilled buttermilk. With your hands, mix to very gently combine all ingredients. (You want it barely combined. Lumps and bumps are okay.) **Note:** The dough will be very sticky, and so will your hands. When you have finished mixing, wash your hands and dry them completely.

Prepare a lightly floured surface. Turn your dough onto your surface. Lightly sprinkle flour all over the top of the dough. Gently fold the dough onto itself about six times. No rolling pin or flattening required; just fold over and over about six times.

Carefully pat the dough into a round about 1 inch thick. Using a 2-inch biscuit cutter or drinking glass, cut biscuits straight down. *Do not* turn or twist your biscuit cutter (this will ensure that you end up with beautiful, fluffy layers). Re-fold and reshape any scraps.

Place biscuits on a baking sheet. Bake for 15 to 20 minutes, or until the tops are lightly golden.

Gravy:

This gravy isn't the rich brown sauce you remember from Thanksgiving. It's a quick and easy white gravy, flavored with pepper. Feel free to add additional pepper for an extra kick!

¼ cup vegetable oil

6 tablespoons flour

1 teaspoon salt

1 ½ teaspoons black pepper

2 cups unsweetened soy milk

Heat vegetable oil in a large skillet over medium-high heat, then whisk in the flour, salt, and pepper. Stir over medium-high heat until completely mixed. Gradually whisk in soy milk and bring the heat to high. The gravy will seem very thin, but keep stirring; it will thicken very quickly. Once the gravy is thick, remove it from the heat. If the gravy is too thick, do not add water; slowly add more soy milk and stir until it reaches the desired consistency.

Alice Leonard

Business Name: Angel Food

Web Site / Location: www.angelfood.co.nz; Auckland, New Zealand

What motivated you to start your business?

I wanted to raise the profile and attractiveness of veganism, because I see this lifestyle as a relatively easy solution to so many huge problems!

What's the most rewarding part of running a vegan business?

I love that every ounce of energy I put into earning a living is also going into promoting veganism!

Do you incorporate green practices in to your work?

Absolutely. Environmental considerations are part of every decision I make in the business. Unfortunately, it's easy to theorize about and not always so easy to practice. For example, I import some products from the other side of the world, which is far from ideal. My reasoning is that veganism is ultimately a more eco-friendly diet, and if importing products like Cheezly from the UK and condensed soya milk from Brazil can help more people make that transition, then I'll do it.

What's your favorite item that you sell?

That would have to be my make-your-own marshmallow and meringue mixes.

Favorite vegan meal?

The tofu and eggplant hotpot at The Golden Age in Victoria St. West, Auckland.

PB AND J MUFFINS BY CELINE STEEN

Yields 12 muffins.

Celine, the lovely lady behind 500 Vegan Recipes *and the* Have Cake, Will Travel *blog, created these PB and J muffins, a delicious take on everyone's favorite sandwich. These hearty muffins can be made with jam, or if you're feeling like a fluffernutter, make them with vegan Ricemellow Creme and nix the orange extract.*

1 cup soy or nondairy milk

1 tablespoon apple cider vinegar

¾ cup Sucanat

½ cup peanut butter

½ cup nondairy yogurt

½ teaspoon sea salt

1 ½ teaspoons vanilla

1 ½ teaspoons orange extract

2 cups whole wheat pastry flour

1 cup old-fashioned oats

2 teaspoons baking powder

1 teaspoon baking soda

Photo Credit: Celine Steen

¼ cup orange jam, divided, or ¼ cup vegan marshmallow cream, such as Ricemellow Creme

Preheat oven to 350°F. Prepare a standard muffin tin with paper liners. Combine milk, vinegar, Sucanat, peanut butter, yogurt, salt, and extracts until emulsified. Add flour, oats, baking powder, and baking soda on top. Fold dry ingredients into wet, being careful not to overmix. Place about 2 tablespoons of batter in each paper liner. Make a little well in the center of each muffin, and place 1 teaspoon jam or marsh-mallow cream in each well. Top with the remaining batter, dividing it among all the muffins. The batter will reach the top of the liner.

Bake for 22 to 24 minutes, until golden brown and firm. Remove from pan and place onto a wire rack. Let cool completely before storing.

BANANA BREAD FRENCH TOAST WITH STRAWBERRY SYRUP

Yields 10 to 12 pieces.

Inspired by a dish I enjoyed on a trip to New York City, I wanted to make my own version of this decadent brunch offering. While this can take a bit of time, if you make the bread and syrup the night before, you'll have French toast in no time the next morning. *The banana bread is good on its own, but it's really designed to be battered and fried for maximum deliciousness! If you don't want to make the syrup, this is just as good with maple syrup.*

Banana Bread:

2 cups very ripe bananas

1 cup sugar

⅓ cup canola oil

1 tablespoon molasses

1 ½ teaspoons vanilla

1 ½ cups all-purpose flour

1 teaspoon baking powder

½ teaspoon baking soda

1 teaspoon salt

½ teaspoon cinnamon

Photo Credit: Hannah Kaminsky

Preheat the oven to 350°F. Lightly grease a 9 x 5 or similar-size loaf pan. In a stand mixer or with a hand mixer, blend the bananas until relatively smooth. Add the sugar, oil, molasses, and vanilla, and mix to combine. Stir in the flour, baking powder, baking soda, salt, and cinnamon, and then pour the mixture into the prepared pan. Bake for 55 to 60 minutes, until a toothpick comes out clean. Allow the bread to cool completely before making French toast, then slice it into ¾-inch pieces.

French Toast Batter:

4 tablespoons flour

1 tablespoon chickpea flour

1 tablespoon cinnamon

A pinch of nutmeg

1 cup nondairy milk (if using unsweetened, add 1 tablespoon sugar plus 1 tablespoon vanilla)

Preheat a pan over medium heat and lightly coat it with oil or vegan margarine. Mix the flour, chickpea flour, cinnamon, and nutmeg in a bowl. Add the nondairy milk slowly, whisking as you go.

Dip the bread in the batter, allowing the excess to fall off, and then add it to the pan. Allow the bread to brown, about 5 minutes per side, then serve warm with strawberry syrup or other topping of choice.

Strawberry Syrup:

1 pound strawberries, hulled and finely diced

¾ cup turbinado sugar

¼ cup lemon juice

¼ teaspoon lemon zest

In a saucepan, combine all the ingredients and then bring to a boil over medium heat. Lower the heat and simmer until the strawberries are soft, about 20 minutes. Mash the berries into the syrup and then either serve as is, or strain the berries and return the syrup to medium heat to reduce for another 10 minutes.

SOUPS AND SALADS

BASIC LENTIL SOUP

Makes 6 servings.

A warm and comforting lentil soup is a staple in most households. Perfect for winter nights or when you're fighting off a cold, this simple dish is perfect with a side of foccacia or crusty bread. I like to use French lentils for their heartiness, but brown lentils can be used as well (take care not to overcook them into mush). This makes a great base recipe, so don't be afraid to experiment with your favorite vegetables and seasonings. The content of salt in vegetable broths varies, so keep that in mind when seasoning your dish.

2 tablespoons olive oil

1 medium onion, diced

2 stalks of celery, diced

2 medium carrots, diced

3 cloves of garlic, minced

1 teaspoon thyme

½ teaspoon to 1 teaspoon salt, to taste

Pepper, to taste

4 cups vegetable broth

1 cup of French lentils, rinsed

1 (14-ounce) can of diced tomatoes

Juice of 1 lemon, about 2 tablespoons

Preheat a soup pot with oil over medium-high heat. Add the onion, carrot, and celery to the pot; sauté until softened and the onion is translucent, 5 to 7 minutes. Add the garlic, thyme, ½ teaspoon salt, and pepper, stirring to combine. Pour in the broth, lentils, and tomatoes; cover the pot and bring it to a boil. Once boiling, reduce the heat to low and simmer covered for 30 to 35 minutes, or until the lentils have softened. Remove from heat, and add the lemon juice, along with salt and pepper to taste. Serve hot!

CHIPOTLE HOMINY STEW

Makes 4 to 6 servings.

This warmly spiced Mexican stew gets a bit of zip from the chipotle peppers, and is full of chewy hominy and beans with a kick of lime. It's a great dish to feed to anyone, vegan or not, and can be dressed up with an array of delicious toppings.

1 tablespoon olive oil

1 medium red onion, diced

4 cloves garlic, minced

1 teaspoon salt

1 teaspoon black pepper

1 teaspoon ground cumin

1 tablespoon epazote or oregano

1 to 3 teaspoons adobo sauce from canned chipotles, based on your spice preference

1 chipotle chile, finely diced

1 (29-ounce) can of prepared hominy, drained and rinsed

1 (14-ounce) can of pinto beans, drained and rinsed

1 (28-ounce) can of diced tomatoes, preferably in juice

Photo Credit: Hannah Kaminsky

28 ounces of water

Juice of 1 lime, 3 to 4 tablespoons

Garnish options:

Chopped cilantro

Radishes, thinly sliced

Diced avocado

Shredded lettuce

Crushed tortilla chips

Nondairy sour cream

In a 5-quart saucepan, heat the oil over medium heat. Add the onion and cook for 3 to 5 minutes, or until translucent. Add the garlic, cook for 2 minutes, then add salt, pepper, cumin, epazote, chipotle in adobo, and diced chipotle. Stir to combine. Add the pinto beans and hominy, and then add the can of diced tomatoes. Fill the can with water, add it to the pot, and stir to combine. Cover and bring to a boil, then reduce the heat and simmer for 10 minutes, partially covered. After 10 minutes, add the lime juice. Allow the stew to sit for 5 to 10 minutes to combine the flavors. Taste for seasoning, then divide among soup bowls and garnish as desired.

BROCCOLI MISO CHOWDER

Makes 4 servings.

This broccoli soup has a twist that gives it a depth of flavor—plus it's incredibly easy to make! If you're inexperienced with miso, err on the side of 3 tablespoons; you can always add more at the end.

1 tablespoon olive oil

1 medium onion, diced

3 cloves of garlic, minced

2 carrots, finely diced

1 pound broccoli, stems and florets separated and chopped

1 teaspoon black pepper

3 cups vegetable broth

3 to 4 tablespoons mellow white miso

½ cup of warm water

½ teaspoon nutmeg

½ teaspoon sea salt (optional)

Heat a stockpot with oil over medium-high heat. Sauté the onions for 5 to 7 minutes, until translucent and starting to brown, and then add the garlic. Add the carrots and broccoli stems and cook until they begin to soften, about 5 minutes. Season with salt and pepper, then add the broccoli florets. Add 3 cups of vegetable broth, cover the pot, and bring to a boil. Once boiling, reduce the heat to medium-low, cover the pot, and allow to simmer for 25 minutes, stirring occasionally.

Dissolve 3 tablespoons of miso paste in ½ cup of warm water and set aside. Once the carrots and broccoli have softened, about 25 minutes later, remove from heat. Add the miso mixture and nutmeg. Use an immersion blender to puree the soup until smooth. Taste for flavor, and then add the final tablespoon of miso and salt, if desired.

Allow to sit for 10 minutes to develop the flavor. Taste for salt and pepper, and then serve immediately.

A WORD ABOUT GARLIC

Yes, garlic can scare away a vampire, but it can also add tons of flavor to a dish. In these recipes, I used big, plump California garlic cloves, which are about 1 inch long and ½ inch thick. If your garlic cloves are smaller, consider using more than the recipe outlines, especially if you're a garlic fan.

SPINACH STRAWBERRY SALAD WITH MAPLE TEMPEH CROUTONS BY TERRY HOPE ROMERO

Serves 2 huge entree portions or 4 smaller starter salads.

If you don't know the name Terry Hope Romero, you should! Terry is the coauthor of favorite vegan cookbooks: Veganomicon, Vegan Cupcakes Take Over the World, *and* Vegan Cookies Invade Your Cookie Jar. *As a solo author, Terry has just released her newest showstopping book focusing on Latin cuisine, called* Viva Vegan. *All of the above are musts for your cookbook collection.*

I love this salad of fresh greens, bright strawberries, and crunchy toasted pecans. You can taste springtime in every bite! Seek out the mild, easy-to-slice, finger-shaped French breakfast radishes for a crisp, fresh complement to the mix. It's a whole farmers' market in a salad bowl, and smoky sweet tempeh "croutons" lend a hearty protein boost to this entree salad.

Busy chefs may want to marinate the tempeh up to 8 hours in advance; roast and then chop the pecans; make the dressing; and store everything in separate, tightly covered containers. Prep the salad ingredients in the morning: Clean and dry the spinach, greens, onions, and radishes, and store them in a large sealed plastic bag, keeping it well chilled. All that's left to do, just 20 minutes before serving, is to cook the tempeh and slice the strawberries right before tossing everything together.

1 (8-ounce) package tempeh

Marinade:

¼ cup fresh-squeezed orange juice

2 tablespoons light soy sauce

   (avoid strong soy sauce, such as tamari)

2 tablespoons maple syrup

1 tablespoon lemon juice

1 tablespoon peanut or grapeseed oil

1 ¼ teaspoons liquid smoke

Peanut or canola oil for pan-frying

Dressing:

2 tablespoons grapeseed oil

1 tablespoon white wine vinegar

1 teaspoon agave nectar

salt and freshly ground pepper to taste

Salad:

1 pound spinach leaves, torn into bite-size pieces

2 generous handfuls of arugula or favorite spring salad greens

Photo Credit: Nicole Carpenter

1 pint strawberries, hulled, washed, and patted dry

1 cup thinly sliced mild radishes

1 small red onion, peeled and sliced into thin rings

½ cup toasted pecans, coarsely chopped

Remove tempeh from packaging and slice cake in half, lengthwise. Slice entire tempeh cake into quarters. Add about 5 inches of water to a large pot, cover, and bring to a boil. Use tongs to lower tempeh into boiling water and cook for about 8 minutes, or until softened and slightly plumped. Remove tempeh and cool for 5 minutes on a dinner plate. Tempeh can also be microwaved in a covered glass micro-wave-safe bowl by covering with 3 inches of water and cooking on high for 6 minutes, until soft; then drain off water.

In a shallow baking dish or pie plate, whisk together marinade ingredients. Dice cooled tempeh into ½-inch cubes, add to marinade, and gently stir to coat each piece. Let sit for 10 minutes, occasionally swirling around the dish to further coat with marinade; set aside. Whisk together dressing ingredients in a measuring cup. Use a salad spinner to wash and dry spinach and greens, then place in a large salad serving bowl. Slice cleaned strawberries into ¼-inch-thick slices and add to salad, along with radishes, onion, and pecans.

Fifteen minutes prior to serving, cook the tempeh. Preheat a 10-inch cast-iron skillet over medium heat; generously coat the bottom with peanut or canola oil.

Add half of the marinated tempeh, taking care not to crowd the pan. Cook for 3 minutes until golden brown, then use a spatula to flip the pieces in order to brown the other side. Spoon some of the marinade over the cooking tempeh. Cook for 6 to 8 minutes, flipping once or twice more until tempeh cubes are well browned. Use the spatula to move cooked tempeh to a plate. Coat the pan with another thin layer of oil and repeat the process with the remaining tempeh, sprinkling cooking cubes with remaining marinade.

When tempeh has finished cooking, add hot tempeh cubes to the salad and pour on the dressing. Use large tongs to toss the salad, gently grabbing the ingredients but thoroughly coating each salad element with dressing, and serve.

TANGY CABBAGE BEET SLAW

Makes 8 servings.

If you would have told me when I was a teenage vegetarian that I would one day enjoy a salad with beets, I would have laughed in your face. I probably would have liked this dish back then, but there's no way I would have tried it, knowing it was full of raw beets. These days I find I'm open to trying foods I would have shunned during my youth, and thankfully, it has resulted in recipes like this delicious slaw with a kick from Dijon mustard. This is great picnic or potluck fare since it's best when made in advance, and can be served cold or at room temperature.

1 large cabbage head, 5 to 6 cups, cored and cut into thin strips

3 small beets or 1 large beet, about 1 ½ cups, grated

2 medium carrots, about 2 cups, grated

⅓ cup red wine vinegar

3 tablespoons olive oil

2 tablespoons Dijon mustard

2 teaspoons agave or 1 ¼ teaspoons sugar

Salt and pepper, to taste

In a small bowl, whisk together the vinegar, oil, sweetener, a pinch of salt, and the pepper. Place the cabbage, beets, and carrots in a large bowl and mix to combine. Pour the dressing over the mixture and stir, making sure to coat everything. If needed, season with salt and pepper, then serve right away. Or for best results, place the slaw in the refrigerator for at least one hour, allowing the flavors to meld. Stir again before serving, either cold or at room temperature.

Tip: For ease, assemble the salad in a 1-gallon plastic bag. Seal the bag, shake to combine, then press the air out and refrigerate it with heavy objects on top. Transfer to a bowl before serving.

AUSTRIAN POTATO SALAD

Makes 4 to 6 servings.

Tangy and creamy potato salad, without the vegan mayonnaise! My friend Megan insisted I include this recipe in the book after I brought it to a potluck, so here it is. In Vienna, I noticed they love their potatoes, and this salad is what you'll often find alongside schnitzel or sausages (vegan versions, of course). This is a great potluck dish to serve to anyone; they'll never miss the mayo!

- 1 pound potatoes, red or Yukon gold, roughly peeled, and cut into ½-inch-thick pieces
- 1 cup vegetable broth
- 1 teaspoon sugar
- ½ teaspoon salt
- 1 tablespoon white wine vinegar, divided
- 1 tablespoon Dijon mustard
- 2 tablespoons canola or vegetable oil
- 1 small red onion, finely minced
- 8 to 10 cornichons or gherkins, finely minced
- Pepper, to taste

In a large, flat-bottomed skillet, bring the potatoes, broth, sugar, salt, and 1 ½ teaspoons of vinegar to a boil. Reduce the heat to low, cover, and simmer for 15 minutes, or until the potatoes are tender. Remove the lid and turn the heat to high for 2 minutes, allowing the liquid to reduce. Reserve ⅓ cup of the liquid, then drain the potatoes. In the reserved liquid, add the mustard, oil, and remaining vinegar. Whisk together, then mash in ¼ cup cooked potatoes to form a thick, chunky sauce.

In a large bowl, combine the potatoes, onion, and cornichons; then add the sauce and carefully fold everything together. Season with pepper, taste for salt, and serve warm or at room temperature. For additional color, try garnishing the salad with freshly chopped chives.

SIDE DISHES

TWICE-BAKED CHIPOTLE SWEET POTATOES

Yields 8 halves.

Spicy and sweet, these twice-baked potatoes are a delicious side dish to accompany just about any meal. If you roast the sweet potatoes in advance, you can get these to the table in 30 minutes. Spice lovers can add more adobo sauce or another pureed pepper if they want a fire in their mouth.

4 large sweet potatoes, about 2 ½ pounds

1 canned chipotle pepper (in adobo), pureed

2 teaspoons adobo sauce from the can of chipotles

2 tablespoons Earth Balance or other vegan margarine

Photo Credit: Nicole Carpenter

2 tablespoons lime juice

1 teaspoon salt

½ teaspoon ground pepper

Preheat oven to 400°F. Place the sweet potatoes on a foil-lined baking sheet and bake in the oven until soft, 45 to 60 minutes. Remove the potatoes from the oven and let them cool until you are able to handle them. Slice potatoes in half lengthwise and scoop out the flesh, taking care not to break the skin. Turn the oven down to 350°F. Add the chipotle pepper to a food processor with the sweet potato flesh, adobo sauce, Earth Balance, lime juice, salt, and pepper, and puree until smooth. Taste the mixture and season as needed.

Fill each of the skins, then place the halves back on the baking sheet and bake for 15 to 20 minutes, until tops are lightly browned. Remove the sweet potato skins from the oven and serve warm.

ROASTED BALSAMIC CAULIFLOWER AND CANNELLINI BEANS

Makes 2 to 4 servings.

Crispy roasted cauliflower paired with creamy cannellini beans make an excellent combination. This is a super simple side containing a little punch from the balsamic vinegar.

1 medium head of cauliflower, about 4 to 5 cups, cut in small florets

1 (15-ounce) can of cannellini beans, drained and rinsed

2 tablespoons olive oil

2 tablespoons balsamic vinegar

3 cloves of garlic, minced

1 teaspoon rosemary, crumbled

½ teaspoon salt

Pepper, to taste

Photo Credit: Nicole Carpenter

Preheat the oven to 400°F. In a bowl, whisk together the oil, vinegar, garlic, rosemary, salt, and pepper. Add the beans and cauliflower to the bowl and toss to coat. Spread the mixture in a single layer in a roasting pan or on a baking sheet. Bake for 30 to 35 minutes, stirring halfway through, until the beans are slightly crispy and the cauliflower is tender and browned. Sprinkle with a pinch of salt and serve.

ASPARAGUS ALMONDINE

Makes 2 to 4 servings.

This is an insanely simple but amazingly flavorful way to prepare these lovely green stalks of yum! This dish is a perfect side to a Thanksgiving feast, or for a night on the couch nestled up with some seitan and gravy. I debated adding spices to this, but really, it's delicious as is, and ready in just 10 minutes.

¼ cup slivered almonds

1 tablespoon olive oil

1 pound asparagus, fibrous ends trimmed, stalks cut in half

¼ teaspoon salt

1 tablespoon lemon juice

In a large skillet, toast the slivered almonds until lightly browned; set aside.

Over medium heat, coat the bottom of the skillet with oil, and then add the asparagus. Sauté the asparagus until crisp-tender, about 5 minutes, depending on stalk thickness. Put a lid over the skillet and allow to steam for 2 minutes. Sprinkle with salt and lemon juice, stir to coat, and then remove from heat. To serve, spread the asparagus over a platter and sprinkle with the toasted almonds.

SWISS CHARD AND POTATO GRATIN

Yields 4 to 6 servings.

Potatoes au gratin, scalloped potatoes—many of us grew up on creamy potato dishes that hovered somewhere between delicious and stomach turning. Luckily, this one is clearly on the winning team and gets a boost of healthiness from Swiss chard without sacrificing the creaminess.

1 tablespoon oil

1 medium onion, sliced in half moons

2 cloves of garlic, minced

½ teaspoon thyme, crumbled

1 bunch of Swiss chard, about 1 pound

½ teaspoon salt

½ pound potatoes, sliced in ⅛- to ¼-inch-thick rounds

Photo Credit: Hannah Kaminsky

Sauce:

2 tablespoons canola or vegetable oil

2 tablespoons flour

1 ¼ cups unsweetened nondairy milk

¼ teaspoon ground mustard

¼ teaspoon salt

¼ teaspoon pepper

pinch of nutmeg

Topping:

2 tablespoons panko (Japanese) breadcrumbs

1 tablespoon nutritional yeast

Preheat the oven to 400°F and lightly grease a 9 x 9 glass dish or casserole pan. Cut the chard in ¼-inch pieces from the stem up to the top of the leaves. Heat the oil in a deep skillet over medium heat. Add the onion and sauté until translucent, about 5 minutes. Stir in the garlic and thyme and then add the chard, a handful at a time, stirring until combined. When all of the chard has been added, sprinkle salt over it. Raise the heat to high and continue to sauté for about 5 to 7 minutes, until the greens are wilted. Remove from heat and set aside.

Sauce:

In a saucepan, heat the oil over low heat. Slowly add the flour while continuously whisking, making sure to avoid lumps. Stir for about 2 minutes, taking care not to burn the mixture; a paste should form. Continue to whisk, adding the milk in a slow, steady stream. Once combined, allow the mixture to simmer on low, stirring occasionally, for 5 to 7 minutes. The sauce should be thickened, but thin enough to spread. Turn off the heat and stir in the seasoning.

Place a layer of potatoes, slightly overlapping, along the bottom of the baking pan. Add half of the chard mixture over the potatoes, and then half the sauce. Make another layer with the rest of the potatoes, then chard, then sauce. Cover with a lid or foil and bake until it is bubbling and the potatoes are softened, about 25 to 30 minutes.

Remove the gratin and turn the oven to broil. Remove the lid or foil from the potatoes, and then combine the breadcrumb and nutritional yeast topping. Sprinkle the topping on the gratin in an even layer. Return to the oven uncovered and place under the broiler for 1 to 2 minutes, until the top is lightly browned. Serve hot.

STRAWBERRY BASIL RISOTTO

Makes 4 servings.

While strawberries in a risotto may sound like a strange dessert, this dish is actually savory with a very light sweetness. Underripened berries work best here, so save those sweet peak-season morsels for another time. It is crucial that your vegetable broth is warm, so don't skip this! This dish may give your arms a workout, but your belly will reap all the benefits. While I'm not sure that this risotto would be Gordon Ramsey–approved, I do feel confident that this unique dish won't be sent back to your kitchen.

Photo Credit: Hannah Kaminsky

1 cup unripened strawberries, hulled and roughly chopped

1 tablespoon balsamic vinegar

1 cup Arborio rice

2 tablespoons olive oil, divided

4 medium shallots, finely diced

4 cups of hot vegetable broth,

¼ cup reserved

8 to 10 large leaves of basil, cut in thin strips

Salt and pepper, to taste

Place the strawberries in a bowl, mix with the balsamic vinegar, and set aside.

Heat a large, heavy-bottomed pot over low, then add the dry Arborio rice and toast for 4 minutes, stirring occasionally, taking care not to brown it. Remove the rice from the heat and set aside.

Place the large, heavy-bottomed pot over medium heat with 1 tablespoon of the oil. Add shallots and sauté until translucent and starting to brown, 3 to 5 minutes. Pour the strawberry mixture (including the liquid) into the pot. Sauté the berries for 2 minutes, allowing them to soften. Add the rice and stir for 1 minute, making sure to coat everything evenly. Add ½ cup of hot vegetable broth and stir, until the broth has been absorbed. Continue to add broth, ½ cup at a time, stirring as it absorbs, until only ¼ cup is left.

After 20 to 25 minutes, the broth should be mostly absorbed, and the rice should be cooked al dente, and not mushy. Place the basil, ¼ cup of remaining broth, 1 table-spoon oil, salt, and pepper in the pot, stir for 1 minute, then remove from heat. Allow the risotto to thicken and the flavors to meld for 5 minutes. Taste and serve, garnished with a strawberry and some chopped basil.

MUSTARD GREENS SAAG

Makes 2 to 4 servings.

You need to eat your greens, so why not go for an Indian spiced curry, also known as saag? Make yourself an Indian feast by pairing this with the Matar Tofu (recipe on page 167) and rounding it out with rice or roti.

1 bunch mustard greens, removed from the stem and torn into small pieces

1 bunch of spinach, about 4 ounces, stems removed, leaves torn into small pieces

1 cup of water

½ teaspoon salt

1 tablespoon oil

1 small onion, diced

3 cloves of garlic

1 teaspoon coriander

1 teaspoon cumin

1 teaspoon garam masala

1 tablespoon lemon juice

Place the mustard greens, spinach, water, and salt in a pot, bring to a boil, then lower the heat and simmer until cooked, about 5 minutes.

Preheat a skillet over medium heat, add the oil, then sauté the onion until translucent, about 5 to 7 minutes. Add garlic, coriander, cumin, and garam masala, and stir the spices to coat everything. Add the lemon juice to deglaze the pan, and then remove the skillet from the heat. Transfer the onion mixture into the pot of cooked spinach. Using an immersion blender, blend the spinach and onion until you have a thick paste, leaving some texture. Taste for seasoning and serve hot.

ENTREES

PASTA WITH ASPARAGUS IN LEMON CREAM SAUCE

Makes 6 servings.

Who needs dairy-laden pasta when you can make your own creamy version with cashews? This simple recipe makes for a great dinner, as it comes together quickly and uses fresh asparagus for a bit of green. When asparagus isn't in season, try broccoli.

1 pound pasta noodles, spaghetti or fettuccine

1 tablespoon olive oil

3 to 4 cloves of garlic, minced

½ to 1 teaspoon red pepper flakes, to taste

1 pound asparagus stalks, cut into 1-inch pieces

½ teaspoon salt

Lemon Cream Sauce:

1 cup raw cashews

1 ¼ cups water

3 tablespoons lemon juice

Zest of 1 lemon

1 teaspoon salt

½ teaspoon pepper

Prepare the pasta according to the package directions; drain and set aside. While the pasta is cooking, prepare the lemon cream sauce. In your food processor, add the cashews and puree for a few minutes until a smooth paste forms. Add the zest, salt, and pepper, and blend again. Pour in the lemon juice and water in a steady stream; process until smooth. The sauce should be thin.

In a deep skillet, heat the oil over medium heat. Stir in garlic and red pepper, then add the asparagus and sprinkle on the salt. Sauté the asparagus until crisp but tender, about 5 to 7 minutes, depending on the thickness of your stalks. Add the pasta to the skillet, toss to combine, and remove from heat. Pour in the lemon cream sauce; stir to coat. Once everything is coated, taste for seasoning, and serve hot.

BASIC THREE-BEAN CHILI

Makes 4 to 6 servings.

Chili—a food that appeals to omnivores, packs a great protein punch, and is just as at-home at a summer cookout as it is in a snowstorm in the dead of winter. This is a great way to feed your family of anti-vegans without the Twenty Questions game, as it's bulked up with beans and doesn't contain any sort of "weird" meat substitute. This chili is also full of pantry staples, so you can make it with grocery-store supplies when you visit your second cousin in the depths of the desert, or when you're hiding out at a cabin in the mountains. Look at this as your basic chili, and don't be afraid to experiment with this recipe. I've added some variations at the end to get you started!

1 tablespoon olive oil

1 medium onion, diced

1 medium carrot, diced

3 cloves of garlic, minced

1 tablespoon mild chile powder

2 teaspoons cumin

2 teaspoons oregano

1 teaspoon salt

1 (15-ounce) can of kidney beans, drained and rinsed

1 (15-ounce) can of pinto beans, drained and rinsed

1 (15-ounce) can of black beans, drained and rinsed

1 (15-ounce) can of diced tomatoes

1 (15-ounce) can tomato sauce

¼ cup water

1 cup corn, fresh or frozen

Preheat a large deep pot with oil over medium heat. Sauté the onion, carrot, and garlic until the onions are translucent and the vegetables start to soften, about 5 minutes. Add the chile powder, cumin, oregano, and salt, stirring to combine. Add the beans, tomatoes, sauce, and water, and raise the heat. Once boiling, reduce the heat to medium-low, cover the pot, and allow to simmer for 15 minutes. Add the corn and partially cover, allowing the mixture to simmer for 5 to 8 minutes. If using fresh corn, simmer for 8 to 10 minutes. Remove from the heat, taste for seasoning, and enjoy!

Variations:

Spicy Chili: Add ½ teaspoon red pepper flakes to the onion and garlic mixture, and ¼ to ½ teaspoon cayenne pepper to the spices.

Hearty Vegetable Chili: Add 1 diced bell pepper, 1 minced stalk of celery, 1 diced zucchini, and 1 tablespoon of oil to the onion and garlic mixture. If needed, add ¼ cup more water with the tomato and bean mixture.

Smoky Chipotle Chili: Add 1 finely chopped chipotle pepper, 1 teaspoon adobo sauce, and 1 teaspoon liquid smoke to the tomatoes and beans.

BRUSSELS SPROUTS WITH CRISPY TEMPEH OVER SOFT POLENTA

Makes 4 servings.

This is a relatively quick but flavorful dish, great for a weeknight when you need a balanced meal with little fuss. Even Brussels sprouts haters will be pleasantly surprised by this, so don't knock it before you try it! For the fastest preparation, prepare the tempeh seasoning, slice the vegetables, and then crisp the tempeh. Meanwhile, start the polenta, and then proceed with the rest of the recipe.

Crispy Tempeh:

- 8 ounces of tempeh, sliced very thin (at least 24 pieces)
- 2 tablespoons soy sauce
- 1 tablespoon olive oil
- 1 tablespoon maple syrup
- 1 tablespoon balsamic vinegar
- 2 cloves of garlic, crushed
- ½ teaspoon liquid smoke
- 1 teaspoon mild chile powder
- ½ teaspoon cumin
- ¼ teaspoon black pepper

Photo Credit: Hannah Kaminsky

Rithika Ramesh

Business Name: The Green Stove

Web Site / Location: http://www.facebook.com/pages
/The-Green-Stove/308206814685; Mumbai, India

What motivated you to start your business?

I've always loved to cook. I remember being in the kitchen with my great-grandmother and grandmother when I was six. After working on films for a few years, I decided that I wanted to do something I really liked. That's about the time I went vegan, and also realized that I could finally do something I liked while also doing my bit for nature and for the animals. It couldn't get any better.

Do you put an emphasis on the vegan aspect of the company, and, if so, do you find that it works in your favor?

I absolutely place emphasis on the vegan aspect of the company, because it is important for me to spread the vegan message among both vegans

and non-vegans that vegan food is not necessarily restrictive. People are very touchy when it comes to food choices, so I prefer placing emphasis on the fact that vegan food is a healthier option, rather than getting into the stories of animal cruelty that cause people to become defensive. I think it works in my favor because many people are somewhat aware that there is something fundamentally wrong with what they are eating; they know that they're addicted to it, and they don't think they have the willpower to avoid these harmful foods.

How do you handle any animosity toward veganism in your personal life or business?

Coming from a country that welcomes vegetarianism as a part of religion, you would think it would be easy, but people are still hung up on old ideas about milk and its production. Initially when I went vegan, I was too excited for my own good, and may have been overly aggressive when discussing it with others, but now if I find people questioning my choice, I let them ask questions and answer calmly. I've realized that if I confidently answer their questions, it makes them think about it, and they will ask more questions.

Favorite vegan meal?

To cook at home: Pasta in pesto with cashew cream.

Dining out: If you're in Mumbai, you have to love Paani Puri; hollow balls of flour stuffed with potatoes and sprouts, dipped in sweet, tangy, and spicy chutneys.

Combine all of the ingredients in a shallow pan, covering each side of the tempeh, and then allow to marinate while you chop the Brussels sprouts and onion. Preheat a deep skillet over medium heat and spray it with a light coating of oil. Add the tempeh strips, reserving the marinade, and cook until very crispy, about 5 to 7 minutes on each side. Remove the tempeh from the skillet and set aside. If the skillet is completely blackened, carefully add a few splashes of water, scrape the blackened pieces, and discard them.

Brussels Sprouts:

1 tablespoon olive oil

1 small onion, sliced

1 pound Brussels sprouts, stems cut and sliced in half

1 teaspoon salt

½ teaspoon black pepper

Leftover tempeh seasoning

½ cup water

Reheat the skillet over medium heat, add the oil, and sauté the onion until it begins to soften, 3 to 5 minutes. Add the Brussels sprouts and sauté for 5 minutes, making sure to brown the cut side, then add the salt and pepper.

In the pan with the remaining tempeh seasoning, add ½ cup water, and then add it to the pan with the Brussels sprouts. Cover, reduce to medium-low heat, and allow to simmer for 7 minutes. Remove the lid and continue to cook for 3 minutes, or until the liquid has absorbed and the mixture has started to look dry. Turn off the heat and taste for seasoning.

Soft Polenta:

5 cups of water, divided

1 teaspoon salt

1 cup polenta

1 tablespoon nutritional yeast

1 tablespoon almond butter

Dash of pepper

Bring 4 cups of water and 1 teaspoon salt to a boil, and then reduce the heat to low. Whisk in the polenta and allow to simmer. After 5 minutes, whisk in 1 more cup of water and continue to simmer, stirring occasionally, for 10 minutes. Stir in the nutritional yeast, almond butter, and a dash of pepper, then remove from heat.

To assemble: Place a generous portion of polenta on a plate, top with the Brussels sprouts mixture, and crumble tempeh over the top. Serve warm.

MAC 'N' CHEESIE CASSEROLE BY KITTEE BERNS

Makes 6 to 8 servings as an entree, more as a side dish.

Kittee's smoky, spicy, cheesy noodle casserole is a great accompaniment for Southern-style dishes. Luckily, Kittee is the master of vegan New Orleans cuisine and has a book coming out in the future, so you'll soon have a supply of recipes to complement this one. To keep it gluten-free, simply use a wheat-free tamari and brown rice pasta, which has protein and a great texture. Nobody will even notice the difference.

16 ounces (1 pound) pasta elbows

1 cup raw cashew pieces

3 cups water

½ cup oat flour

2 tablespoons chickpea flour

2 tablespoons Earth Balance or other vegan margarine

1 tablespoon olive oil

1 teaspoon chipotle chili powder

1 tablespoon tamari or soy sauce

¼ teaspoon liquid smoke

1 ½ teaspoons smoked salt

Dash of turmeric

¾ cup nutritional yeast

Smoked paprika

Sweet paprika

In a blender, soak the cashews and water for 1 to 3 hours. Blend until perfectly smooth, about 3 minutes, to make cashew milk. Preheat oven to 350°F and prepare the pasta according to package directions; drain.

In a dry saucepan, toast the flours over medium heat for 1 to 2 minutes, until they become slightly fragrant. Add the Earth Balance and oil to the flour mixture and whisk well to make a roux. Reduce heat slightly and stir constantly until the roux is a light peanut-butter color, 3 to 4 minutes. Carefully whisk in the cashew milk, beating vigorously until smooth. Increase heat back to medium and whisk in the chipotle powder, turmeric, liquid smoke, salt, and tamari. Whisk constantly until the sauce just begins to bubble and becomes quite thick. Whisk in the nutritional yeast; beat until smooth and thick, and then remove from heat.

In a deep casserole dish, combine the cooked pasta with all of the sauce except for approximately 1 ½ cups. Mix well to combine. Pour the remaining sauce over the top of the pasta and spread to even out. Sprinkle the top generously with both the smoked and sweet paprika. Bake until hot and bubbly, approximately 30 minutes. If desired, place under the broiler for an additional 1 to 2 minutes to brown the top.

APPLE SAGE RICE STUFFED ACORN SQUASH

Makes 4 servings.

This dish tastes like the holidays, which is exactly what I was going for—a dish you can serve on a special occasion that anyone can enjoy. The rice filling is flavorful and makes a great side on its own, plus you can easily double this recipe so that everyone at the dinner table has their own squash half. This travels well if you plan ahead. Pre-roast the squash and make the rice in advance for fast assembly at your target location.

¾ cup long grain brown rice (or other rice of your choice—but be sure to adjust
   cooking time accordingly)

1 ½ cups water

A pinch of salt

2 acorn squash, halved lengthwise

1 tablespoon olive oil

2 shallots, about ½ cup, roughly chopped

2 celery stalks, diced

1 medium apple (i.e., a Fuji), cut in ¼-inch pieces

1 teaspoon powdered sage

¾ teaspoon salt

¼ teaspoon cinnamon

Pepper, to taste

⅓ cup dried cranberries, roughly chopped

¼ cup hazelnuts, roughly chopped

Preheat the oven to 450°F. In a saucepan with the lid on, bring the rice, water, and a pinch of salt to a boil. Without removing the lid, turn the heat to the lowest setting and allow the rice to simmer for 35 minutes. After turning off the heat, leave the lid on for another 10 minutes. Remove the lid and fluff the rice with a fork.

Prepare the squash by cutting it in half, removing the strings and seeds, then poking the flesh with your knife a few times. Place the squash facedown on a baking sheet and bake for 30 minutes.

While the rice and squash are cooking, prep the ingredients for the rice mixture. Heat a skillet over medium heat and add the oil. Sauté the shallot for 3 to 4 minutes until softened, and then add the celery and apple slices and cook for 5 to 7 minutes, stirring often. Add the spices, stir to coat, and cook for 2 to 3 more minutes before removing it from the heat.

Photo Credit: Nicole Carpenter

Once the rice is done, add it to the skillet and mix everything together.

Remove the squash from the oven, stuff the centers with the rice mixture, cover with foil, and return to the oven. Bake for 15 to 20 minutes until everything is heated through, then serve warm.

MATAR TOFU BY KIP DORRELL

Makes 4 to 6 servings.

Kip Dorrell, the mastermind behind The Messy Vegetarian Cook blog, churns out a range of exciting recipes, such as this one for matar tofu. Who needs paneer when you have tofu? This mildly spiced curry, perfect for both Indian food virgins and those who eschew too much spicy heat, is both simple and delicious. As with most curries, this one only gets better over time, so feel free to make it a day in advance.

8 ounces firm or extra-firm tofu, pressed and cut into ½-inch cubes

2 tablespoons oil

1 (14-ounce) can of tomatoes, whole or diced

1 medium onion, sliced and divided

1 tablespoon tomato paste

1 tablespoon vegetable oil

3 to 4 cloves garlic, minced

2 teaspoons freshly grated ginger

1 bay leaf

½ teaspoon ground cumin

1 teaspoon ground coriander

¼ teaspoon turmeric

¾ teaspoon salt

Cayenne pepper to taste (optional)

1 tablespoon garam masala

¼ to ½ cup water

½ cup unsweetened nondairy milk

2 ½ cups frozen peas

Fresh cilantro, to garnish (optional)

After the tofu has been pressed and cubed, fry over medium-high heat with 1 tablespoon of the oil for about 5 minutes, or until the sides are just beginning to brown lightly (this step helps to seal the tofu so it doesn't crumble in the curry sauce). Remove from the heat and place the tofu on paper towels to remove any excess oil.

Place the canned tomato, tomato paste, and half the onion into a blender or food processor, and blend until smooth.

Add the remaining tablespoon of oil to an extra-large sauté pan or a stockpot and fry the rest of the onion over medium heat, stirring often, for about 10 minutes, or until the onion is translucent and lightly browned, but not burnt. Add the garlic, ginger, and bay leaf, stirring constantly for a minute, then pour in the contents of the blender. Mix the cumin, coriander, turmeric, salt, and chili powder into the sauce. Stir continuously for 12 to 15 minutes, or until the curry sauce thickens slightly and the color deepens a little. Add the nondairy milk, ¼ cup of water, the peas, and the garam masala. Mix to combine well, adding more water if you want a thinner consistency.

Finally, gently stir in the tofu. Turn the heat down marginally, cover, and cook for 20 to 25 minutes. Remove the bay leaf and serve hot, garnished with chopped cilantro if desired.

MOROCCAN CHICKPEA AND KALE TAGINE WITH QUINOA

Makes 6 to 8 servings.

A tagine *is not only a traditional pot made of clay; the word is also used to describe a stew found in North African cuisine. Although this is a less than traditional take, the spices are Moroccan-inspired, while the addition of kale and a bed of quinoa make it modern and two thousand times more vegan. Instead of honey, we add a touch of sweetness with agave nectar, but if you don't have it on hand, it's still good without it.*

Quinoa, kale, and chickpeas are a trifecta of nutrition, so rest easy knowing that this dish is not only delicious, but also good for you!

Tagine:

1 tablespoon olive oil

1 medium onion, diced

3 cloves of garlic, minced

2 medium carrots, cut in ¼-inch rounds

1 ½-inch cinnamon stick, or ¾ teaspoon ground cinnamon

1 bunch of kale, about 8 ounces, cut in strips

2 teaspoons cumin

1 teaspoon ground ginger

½ teaspoon coriander

½ teaspoon paprika

¼ teaspoon cayenne pepper

½ teaspoon salt

¼ teaspoon pepper

1 (14-ounce) can of chickpeas, drained and rinsed

1 (14-ounce) can of diced tomatoes

2 cups vegetable broth

½ cup golden raisins

¼ cup chopped cilantro, divided

¼ cup slivered, toasted almonds

1 tablespoon agave nectar

Quinoa:

1 ½ cups quinoa, rinsed and drained

3 cups water or vegetable broth

Preheat a large stockpot over medium heat, add the oil, then the onion, garlic, carrots, and cinnamon stick. Add the kale in handfuls, stirring to combine each batch. Cover the pot and allow the vegetables to soften for 5 to 7 minutes, stirring occasionally. Add the cumin, ginger, coriander, paprika, cayenne, salt, and pepper; stir for 1 minute, until fragrant. Add the chickpeas, tomatoes, broth, raisins, and 2 tablespoons of the cilantro, then bring to a boil. Cover when boiling and reduce the heat to low and simmer for 10 minutes.

While the tagine simmers, prepare the quinoa. In a small pot, add the quinoa and liquid, then cover and bring to a boil. Turn the heat to low and simmer, covered, until the water is absorbed (about 15 minutes). Remove the quinoa from the heat and keep it covered until ready to serve.

After the tagine has simmered for 10 minutes, remove the lid and simmer uncovered for 10 additional minutes, allowing some of the liquid to absorb. Turn off the heat and stir in the agave nectar, then taste for salt. To serve, put a bed of quinoa on the plate, pour the tagine over the quinoa, and top with cilantro and almonds.

CRACKED CORIANDER SEED AND CHAI TEA–RUBBED VEGAN STEAK LO MEIN BY JENN SHAGRIN

Jenn Shagrin, aka JennShaggy, is the mistress of meaty seitan dishes! On her blog, Veganize It, Don't Criticize It, she tackles everything from Vegan Quattro Formaggio White Truffle Macaroni and Cheese to Candied Masala Yams Coulis Casserole. Her beef-style seitan can be used for a plethora of dishes, but here she uses it for a "steak" lo mein, in a flavorful seasoning rub. This dish takes a bit of extra time, but you'll find it to be worthwhile. For a shortened version, try the lo mein without the vegan steak; it's delicious!

Beef-Style Seitan:

1 cup vital wheat gluten

1 cup water

1 teaspoon No Beef Broth paste (preferably Better than Bouillon brand, not diluted in water)

1 tablespoon MimicCreme, plain soy creamer, or plain soy yogurt

"Beef" Seitan Broth:

8 cups prepared No Beef Broth (8 teaspoons paste diluted in 8 cups water)

6 dried shiitake mushrooms

⅛ cup tamari

1 portobello mushroom cap, chopped

1 tablespoon garlic powder

2 teaspoons onion powder

2 bay leaves

First, add all of the seitan broth ingredients to a large pot and bring to a boil. While it's heating up, using a stand mixer, mix together all of the seitan dough ingredients. Don't overmix; just let the mixer go

Photo Credit: Jenn Shagrin

until it's all combined. The dough should be quite soft. Using your hands, mold the dough into a large ball. Flatten the ball out on a cutting board and use a sharp knife or kitchen shears to cut into six pie-wedge-shaped pieces. Drop into the boiling broth and reduce the heat to a simmer. Let it cook for about 1 hour, stirring every 10 to 15 minutes. Using tongs, remove the "beef" from the broth and place in a colander to drain. Allow the seitan to cool until ready to use.

Cracked Coriander Seed and Chai Tea Rub:

1 batch of vegan beef–style seitan (6 "steaks")

Light sesame oil, enough for coating the steaks

¼ cup chai tea leaves, finely ground

1 tablespoon coriander seeds, cracked

1 ½ teaspoons ground white pepper

Sea salt

In a small bowl, combine the ground chai tea leaves, cracked coriander seeds, and white pepper. Lightly coat each seitan steak with a bit of sesame oil, then sprinkle with a touch of salt. Rub each steak with an equal amount of the tea leaf/coriander blend, then set aside.

Oil a grill pan or large sauté pan well, then heat the pan until it's hot and ready. Grill the steaks on each side for about 4 to 5 minutes until browned and cooked through, then remove from pan and set aside to cool. Once cool enough to handle, slice the steaks on the bias into thin slices and set aside until the lo mein is finished.

Lo Mein:

1 pound spaghetti or soba noodles

½ cup seasoned rice vinegar

2 cloves garlic, minced

½ teaspoon ground ginger

¼ cup soy sauce

2 tablespoons canola (or vegetable) oil

2 cups small broccoli florets

1 pound white button mushrooms, sliced

1 large onion, largely chopped

1 cup sugar snap peas

1 cup prepared No Beef Broth, chilled in the refrigerator

2 tablespoons cornstarch

¼ cup cilantro

1 teaspoon dark sesame oil

1 batch of cracked coriander seed and chai tea–rubbed steak strips

Black sesame seeds

Bring a large pot of salted water to a boil and cook noodles until just al dente. Drain well, toss with a touch of canola oil, and set aside.

In a medium-size bowl, combine the seasoned rice vinegar, garlic, ground ginger, and soy sauce. Set aside. Heat 2 tablespoons of canola oil in a large wok until hot; add the rice vinegar mixture and broccoli. Stir-fry for 2 minutes, then add the mushrooms, onions, and snap peas and sauté until tender.

Combine the chilled No Beef Broth and cornstarch in a small bowl. Pour it into the wok and allow it to cook until thickened. Add in the cooked noodles and toss to combine, allowing the mixture to cook until the noodles are warmed through completely. Remove from heat, toss with fresh cilantro and dark sesame oil, and then serve topped with slices of cracked coriander seed and chai tea–rubbed steak.

THANKSGIVING DINNER CUTLETS

Yields 8 to 10 cutlets.

Want the taste of Thanksgiving dinner without all the hassle of making a giant meal? Try these cutlets for a taste of the holidays packed into a patty! Serve these smothered in gravy, on a dinner roll, or even as-is for a quick and easy nosh any time of the year.

2 tablespoons olive oil

1 small onion, finely minced

½ cup celery, diced

3 cloves of garlic

1 pound extra-firm tofu, drained

1 tablespoon soy sauce

¼ cup nutritional yeast

1 teaspoon rosemary

1 teaspoon thyme

1 teaspoon sage

1 teaspoon salt

½ teaspoon pepper

A pinch of nutmeg

½ cup dried cranberries, minced

1 cup panko breadcrumbs

Photo Credit: Nicole Carpenter

In a skillet over medium heat, sauté the onion, celery, and garlic in the oil until the celery has softened and the onions are translucent and start to brown, about 5 minutes. Remove from heat and set aside. Crumble the tofu into a large bowl, making sure there are no large chunks left. Add the soy sauce, nutritional yeast, rosemary, thyme, sage, salt, pepper, and nutmeg, and then use your hands to combine everything thoroughly. Scrape the contents of the skillet into the bowl, making sure to add any oil that wasn't absorbed. Fold in the cranberries and breadcrumbs, then mix the contents thoroughly with your hands. Form 8 to 10 flat patties, making sure to tightly pack everything together.

Heat the skillet over medium-low heat and lightly spray with oil. Add a few cutlets at a time and cook them for 4 to 6 minutes on each side, until lightly crisped and heated through. Finish cooking all of the cutlets, then serve warm.

JACKFRUIT "CARNITAS" TACOS

Makes 2 to 4 servings.

This recipe appeared on my blog, The Urban Housewife, after a trip to a certain Southern California restaurant with jackfruit on the menu sparked my interest. When served fresh, this South Asian fruit is sweet, with a spiky exterior. In this case, we're using young jackfruit in a can; although it doesn't have much flavor, the texture is quite meaty when cooked. Jackfruit can be found at most Asian or Indian grocers, typically in a green can. (Be sure to get the kind that's packed in water or brine, not syrup.)

Photo Credit: Hannah Kaminsky

2 (20-ounce) cans of young green jackfruit, in brine or water, not syrup

2 tablespoons mild chile powder

1 tablespoon cumin

1 tablespoon oregano

1 teaspoon pepper

½ teaspoon smoked paprika

¼ teaspoon cayenne pepper

1 large onion, diced

4 cloves garlic, minced

12 ounces salsa verde (I like Trader Joe's brand)

Juice from 1 lime

Drain and rinse the jackfruit thoroughly. With your hands, press the moisture out of each piece and add it to your Crock-Pot. Add the chile powder, cumin, oregano, pepper, paprika, and cayenne to the jackfruit, coating each piece. Add the onion and garlic, then cover the seasoned jackfruit with the salsa verde, taking care to cover everything. Add the lime juice, turn the Crock-Pot to low, and let it simmer for 6 to 8 hours.

For cooking on the stovetop: Add the ingredients to a large pot, following the same assembly directions. Bring to a boil, then simmer on low, covered, for at least 1 hour, preferably 2, stirring occasionally. If the mixture sticks, add a bit more salsa verde or water. Some browned bits are fine. When finished, the jackfruit will have changed colors and be slightly moist and browned. I try to cook a fair amount of the liquid out, which gives it a meatier texture.

Serve the jackfruit in tortillas with additional salsa, a squeeze of lime juice, and any other taco toppings you enjoy!

SLOPPY JOES

Makes 4 servings.

Sometimes on cold nights, you want a hearty, filling meal that reminds you of what Mom used to make. Sloppy Joes seem to be a staple in many American households, but with this recipe, we skip the meat without skimping on protein, and go for tempeh instead.

1 tablespoon olive oil

1 small onion, sliced

3 cloves of garlic, minced

8 ounces of tempeh, crumbled

1 red bell pepper, sliced in strips

2 tablespoons mild chile powder

1 teaspoon cumin

½ teaspoon salt

1 (15-ounce) can of tomato sauce

1 tablespoon brown sugar

1 tablespoon yellow mustard

¼ teaspoon liquid smoke (optional)

Photo Credit: Hannah Kaminsky

Preheat a skillet with oil over medium heat; add the onion and sauté for 5 to 7 minutes, until translucent. Add the garlic, then the crumbled tempeh; sauté for 5 minutes until lightly browned. Add the bell pepper, allowing it to soften (about 3 minutes); then add the chile powder, cumin, and salt, stirring to coat. Stir in the tomato sauce, brown sugar, mustard, and liquid smoke; turn the heat down to medium-low. Allow the mixture to simmer, uncovered, until the sauce thickly coats everything, about 12 to 15 minutes. Taste for salt and serve hot on burger buns.

PORTOBELLO BANH MI SANDWICHES

Yields 4 sandwiches.

Banh mi sandwiches, a combination of Vietnamese and French influences, are popular around the globe. While you may be able to find a vegan tofu version at your local shop (without the mayonnaise—and if the pickled vegetables have no fish sauce), they're fun to make yourself with portobello mushrooms providing a meatier texture. While this may seem like a complex recipe, it's actually quite simple, and it's a quick meal if you prepare the vegetables and marinade in advance.

4 sandwich-sized baguettes

Do Chua:

¼ pound carrots (about 1 large carrot), cut into matchsticks

¼ pound daikon radish (about 1 large radish), cut into matchsticks

2 cups warm water

2 tablespoons rice vinegar

1 tablespoon sugar

1 tablespoon salt

Mushroom Marinade:

4 large portobello mush-
   rooms, stems removed and
   sliced in strips

3 tablespoons soy sauce

3 cloves of garlic, minced

1 tablespoon peanut oil

1 tablespoon rice vinegar

1 tablespoon water

½ to 1 teaspoon Sriracha or
hot sauce, to taste

Photo Credit: Hannah Kaminsky

Sesame Soy Spread (optional):

3 tablespoons tahini

3 tablespoons water

1 tablespoon soy sauce

Fillings:

Cucumber slices

Jalapeno slices

Cilantro sprigs

Red onion slices (optional)

Sriracha (optional)

To make the pickled vegetables, place your carrot and daikon pieces into a jar, airtight container, or sealable plastic bag. Combine the water, rice vinegar, sugar, and salt into a bowl, stirring to dissolve everything. Pour this mixture over the vegetables and allow to marinate for at least 1 hour (preferably longer). The longer they marinate, the better they taste.

Arrange the sliced mushrooms in a large baking pan, at least 9 x 13. Add the soy sauce, garlic, oil, rice vinegar, and hot sauce, then toss to coat. Allow to marinate while the vegetables are pickling, or while you are preparing the rest of the ingredients.

To make the spread, combine the ingredients in a food processor and puree until smooth. Preheat a skillet over medium heat; add the mushrooms along with their marinade, and stir to combine. Turn the heat to high and simmer the mushrooms, stirring occasionally. Allow the sauce to thicken and glaze the mushrooms, about 5 to 7 minutes.

To assemble:

Spread the sliced baguette with the sesame soy spread or vegan mayonnaise. Add the mushrooms, and then pile the sandwich with pickled vegetables, cucumber, jalapeno, cilantro, or any other fillings you desire.

DESSERTS

PURPLE COW CUPCAKES BY HANNAH KAMINSKY

Yields 15 cupcakes.

The world is crazy about cupcakes, myself included. From lines around the block at famous bakeries to books and blogs devoted to recipes just for these perfect, single-serving treats, it seems that cupcakes are everywhere you look! Just when you think you've tried every cupcake out there, here comes Hannah Kaminsky, tireless culinary creative and author of My Sweet Vegan, *with something you likely never imagined. These cupcakes, flavored with grape juice and topped with a "melted ice cream" frosting, will have you shunning the purple cow milkshakes that inspired them, in favor of the baked version!*

Grape Cupcakes:

2 cups all-purpose flour

2 tablespoons cornstarch

¼ teaspoon salt

1 teaspoon baking powder

½ teaspoon baking soda

1 (11.5-ounce) can frozen grape juice concentrate, thawed

⅓ cup canola oil

¼ cup plain soy or coconut yogurt

1 teaspoon vanilla extract

Photo Credit: Hannah Kaminsky

Melted Ice Cream Frosting:

3 cups confectioners' sugar

¾ cup Earth Balance, or other vegan margarine

¼ teaspoon salt

1 ½ whole vanilla beans

1 ½ tablespoons plain soy milk

Preheat your oven to 350°F. Line fifteen standard muffin tins with cupcake papers. In a large bowl, sift together the flour, cornstarch, salt, baking powder, and baking soda. Whisk to distribute the dry goods throughout the mixture.

In a separate bowl, stir the grape juice, oil, yogurt, and vanilla together. Pour the wet mixture into the dry, stirring just enough to combine. It's better to leave a few errant lumps than to risk overmixing and ending up with tough cupcakes.

Portion out the batter equally between your prepared cups, filling each about two-thirds to three-quarters of the way full. Bake for 15 to 20 minutes, until a toothpick inserted into the center comes out clean and dry. Let cool completely before frosting.

To make the frosting, place the margarine in your stand mixer and beat briefly to soften. Add in the sugar and salt, and starting on the very lowest speed, turn on the mixer for just a minute to begin incorporating the two. Use a knife to slice the vanilla beans in two down the whole length of the bean, and then scrape out the seeds by dragging the knife down the cut centers. Add the seeds into the mixing bowl, along with the soy milk, and slowly begin to mix again.

Sara Sohn

Business Name: Sweet & Sara

Web Site / Location: www.sweetandsara.com; Long Island City, New York

What motivated you to start your business?

Growing up, I lived on Rice Krispies treats and Choco Pies (Korea's version of a moon pie), and life was good. I became a vegetarian at the age of thirteen, and a year later, vegan. I discovered how cruel life could be when I realized a vegan lifestyle meant no more marshmallows. For me, no more marshmallows meant no more happy days!

For over a decade I waited and waited, hoping someone would present the world with a vegan marshmallow, but nothing happened. I was suffering from s'mores withdrawal, and recognized I wasn't the only one. I could no longer be deprived of my childhood indulgence. I was a woman on a mission, a hungry one, and I was going to create the first vegan marshmallow, and nothing would get in my way. Gluttony was the genesis of Sweet & Sara.

Do you put an emphasis on the vegan aspect of the company, and, if so, do you find that it works in your favor?

Sweet & Sara definitely puts an emphasis on the vegan aspect, and we talk about the benefits of eating vegan wherever and whenever we can (during interviews, food shows, food demos, on our Web site and brochure), as it's our duty to educate others that vegan food is cruelty-free, and can also be fun and delicious. We never speak in a didactic manner, since nothing peeves people more than a preachy vegan. Luckily, our products speak for themselves, and both vegans and non-vegans are sold on them; hearing about the advantages of eating vegan is just an added bonus. There is now less of a stigma associated with

Photo Credit: George Sierzputowski

vegan food, and people are changing the way they eat. Whether it's due to ethical, health, religious, or environmental choices, consumers are steering toward vegan food now more than ever. Sweet & Sara has been thriving, and has recently been acknowledged by respected mainstream media like Food Network, Rachael Ray, CNBC, and Martha Stewart.

What's the most rewarding part of running a vegan business?

Besides getting to eat delectable vegan treats all day long? The most rewarding part of running a vegan business would be, without a doubt, being able to have an influence on the way people eat—getting people to eat fewer animals. It's intoxicating watching people's faces light up when they eat our marshmallows. We get e-mails and calls all the time from customers thanking us for what we do, and how our marshmallows have made them so happy. That's incredibly rewarding! I live, eat, and breathe my business, and I have the great good fortune of waking up every day, delighting people with sweet, scrumptious treats that we produce, where not a single animal was harmed in the making! I seriously have the sweetest job.

Favorite vegan meal?

Ooooh, this is tough. Pizza was the hardest thing to give up when I went vegan, so I always get super-excited and emotional when I get my hands on a thin-crust pizza with Daiya cheese. I do the happy dance! A dish with grilled seitan always gets me animated, and don't get me started on Mom's bi bim bop—it's to die for. Oh, and good ol' french fries are my weakness, so I'll take a side of that, please. Ending the meal with strawberry shortcake would be bliss.

Once the sugar has mostly been stirred in, turn up the speed to high, and whip for about 5 minutes, scraping down the sides as necessary, until light and fluffy. Transfer to a piping bag, or simply use a spatula to apply the frosting to your cupcakes as desired.

CAPPUCCINO CHIP COOKIES BY JULIE HASSON

Yields about 28 large cookies.

Julie Hasson is a cookbook author (her latest book, Vegan Diner, *is due out in 2011), creator of the vegan cooking show,* Everyday Dish TV, *and the woman behind Portland's Native Bowl vegan food cart. Where she finds the time to do everything, I don't know, but she does it all amazingly well. Once again, she knocks my socks off with these cookies; they will make your eyes roll back in your head, and you will most likely refuse to share. Luckily, this makes a decent-size batch, so you just might relent and hook a friend up!*

2 tablespoons flaxseed meal (ground flaxseed), preferably golden

6 tablespoons hot water

3 ½ cups all-purpose flour

1 tablespoon baking powder

1 tablespoon instant coffee

1 tablespoon finely ground espresso

1 ½ teaspoons baking soda

1 teaspoon ground cinnamon

½ teaspoon finely ground salt

⅔ cup canola oil

2 ¼ cups packed brown sugar

⅓ cup soy milk

1 tablespoon pure vanilla

½ teaspoon pure orange oil (optional)

2 cups rolled oats (old-fashioned)

2 cups vegan chocolate chips or chunks

Preheat oven to 350°F. In a small bowl, whisk together flaxseed meal and hot water. Set aside. In a medium bowl, combine flour, baking powder, coffee powder, espresso, baking soda, cinnamon, and salt.

In a large bowl of stand mixer, beat together oil and brown sugar. Add egg replacer and vanilla, beating until smooth. Add the flour mixture to the oil mixture, beating just until mixed. Add soy milk, beating until mixed. Stir in the oats and chocolate chips.

Glauce Lucas

Location: I'm Brazilian, but have lived in Dublin, Ireland, since 2008.

Blog: Food in my Life (foodinmylife .blogspot.com)

Reason You Went Vegan: Ethical reasons. No animal should be treated as an object or product, and after ten years of veganism, I continue to believe that I'm doing the right thing. I'm trying to make this world a better place to live. No, I can't change the world, but I can do something to make it better. Being vegan is not the only thing we can do—far from it—but it is one important thing. I decided that I can eat and use products without causing suffering, without murder. I decided that the taste is not the best reason to choose my food, and it's 100 percent worth it.

Favorite Dish to Cook: I can't pick just one: Brazilian vegan feijoada, Italian vegan frittata, and vegan cupcakes.

Favorite "Accidentally Vegan" Treat: In Italy, there is a vegan "Nutella" from Valsoia. Another favorite treat is Paçoquinha, from Brazil; it's a crushed peanut candy that I love, and it's vegan.

Scoop mixture onto parchment-lined baking sheets; press tops of cookies with your hand to flatten them into discs. Bake in preheated oven for 14 minutes, or until puffed and light golden brown (but still soft to the touch). Let cookies cool on baking sheet completely before removing.

Tip: If you can't find pure orange oil, you can substitute 1 to 2 tablespoons of finely grated orange zest.

CUTE COOKIES!

A great way to show your appreciation for others is with baked goods, and cookies are an easy grab-and-go treat with mass appeal. There are creative ways to package cookies that add an extra-special touch, but you don't have to break the bank. One great way to package cookies is to line up smaller-size cookies in an empty tea box, with a note written on the top flap of the box. I learned this tip from my friend Isa; I love the fact that it not only looks cute, but you're recycling as well. Another great option is to put a jumbo cookie in a paper CD sleeve with a window on the front, like those used to house CDs. Seal them with a sticker or stamp, then pass them out to the people you love for the holidays, as a wedding favor, or just to show you care.

CARAMELLY POPCORN

Makes 4 to 6 servings.

This is the perfect snack for movie-watching on a cold night, or as a tasty treat when your sweet tooth strikes. For extra-decadent caramel corn for bake sales, impressing friends, or gluttony's sake, double the coating ingredients!

½ cup brown sugar

¼ cup (or 2 ounces) of Earth Balance or other vegan margarine

1 tablespoon maple syrup

1 tablespoon brown rice syrup

½ teaspoon vanilla

¼ teaspoon salt

¼ baking soda

Photo Credit: Hannah Kaminsky

3 tablespoons of popcorn kernels, popped, about 4 to 5 cups

½ cup of roasted nuts of your choice, such as peanuts, almonds, or pecans (optional)

Preheat the oven to 250°F. Pop the 3 tablespoons of popcorn and spread it on a large baking sheet covered in parchment paper, making sure to remove unpopped kernels. If adding nuts, spread them out with the popcorn.

In a medium saucepan, bring the brown sugar, margarine, maple syrup, and brown rice syrup to a boil and simmer for 10 minutes, stirring often. After the mixture has deepened in color and thickened, remove from heat; add the vanilla, salt, and baking soda, stirring while it bubbles.

Pour the caramel over the popcorn, stirring quickly to coat everything. Once coated, place it in the oven for 10 minutes, stirring after 5 minutes, and again at the end to even out the coating. Remove from the oven and allow to cool slightly before eating. Leftover popcorn can be stored in an airtight container.

SWEET TATER BREAD BY BIANCA PHILLIPS

Yields 1 loaf.

Quick breads are great as an after-dinner treat or a sumptuous start to your day. Bianca, author of the Vegan Crunk blog and the upcoming book, Cookin' Crunk, *hooks us up with a recipe for tender bread made with sweet potatoes and the favorite nut of the South, pecans (pronounced PEE-cans, not peh-CAWNS, of course).*

2 medium sweet potatoes (to yield 1 ½ cups mashed, cooked sweet potato)

1 cup pecans, cut into small pieces

2 cups whole wheat pastry flour

¾ cup sugar

2 teaspoons baking powder

¾ teaspoon baking soda

¼ teaspoon sea salt

1 teaspoon cinnamon

½ teaspoon ground ginger

1 very ripe banana

¼ cup canola or safflower oil

¼ cup soy milk

Preheat oven to 350°F. Peel and cube sweet potatoes. Bring a pot of water to a

Photo Credit: Bianca Phillips

boil and add potatoes. Cook for about 20 minutes, or until very soft. Drain water and mash potatoes with a fork or potato masher. Measure out 1 ½ cups; set aside.

While the potatoes are boiling, toast the pecans in a dry pan in the oven for 8 minutes; set them aside.

Mix flour, sugar, baking powder, baking soda, salt, cinnamon, and ginger in a large bowl. In a separate bowl, mash banana and sweet potatoes together. Add the oil and soy milk to the potato mixture and combine. Add the sweet potato mixture to the dry ingredients and stir until well combined. Fold in pecans.

Pour into a greased loaf pan and bake for 60 to 70 minutes, or until a toothpick inserted into the center of the loaf comes out clean.

ALMOND-LIME CAKE WITH LIME-ROSEMARY ICING
BY CONSTANZE REICHARDT

Yields 1 Bundt cake.

Almond, lime, and rosemary work together to make a delectable Bundt cake created by Constanze, from the blog, Seitan Is My Motor. Hailing from Germany, Constanze stays true to her roots and gives us a super-flavorful dessert that isn't overly sweet.

Preheat the oven to 325°F. Grease a 9-inch Bundt pan with margarine and dust it with all-purpose flour. Set aside.

Cake:

2 tablespoons ground flaxseeds

6 tablespoons hot water

½ cup Earth Balance or other vegan margarine, softened

1 cup sugar

¼ cup plain soy yogurt

¼ cup lime juice

1 teaspoon ground vanilla, or 2 teaspoons vanilla extract

2 cups all-purpose flour

2 teaspoons baking powder

¼ teaspoon salt

1 cup ground almonds

2 teaspoons lime zest

Photo Credit: Nicole Carpenter

In a small bowl, whisk together flaxseeds and hot water until thickened. Set aside. With a handheld mixer, cream together butter and sugar until light and fluffy (about 5 minutes). Add the flax mixture, yogurt, lime juice, and vanilla. Beat until well combined.

Sift in flour, add baking powder and salt, and mix until combined. The batter will be rather thick and quick-bread-like. Fold in the almonds and lime zest.

Pour the batter into your prepared pan and bake for 45 minutes, or until a toothpick inserted into the center comes out clean. Remove the cake from the oven and let it cool in the pan for at least 20 minutes. Let cool completely before serving.

Icing:

1 cup sifted powdered sugar

4 teaspoons lime juice

¾ tablespoon finely chopped fresh rosemary

½ teaspoon lime zest

Additional lime zest and chopped rosemary for sprinkling

Combine all ingredients in a food processor and process until smooth. Pour over the cake as desired. Lightly sprinkle with lime zest and rosemary.

GIANT BAKERY-STYLE DOUBLE-CHOCOLATE COOKIES BY KELLY PELOZA

Yields 8 to 10 giant cookies (or more small ones).

This recipe comes from the young and talented Kelly Peloza, author of The Vegan Cookie Connoisseur. *I tested recipes for her book in 2006, when she was only seventeen, and was surprised by how delicious her cookie recipes are, and what a great understanding she has for the science of baking. These cookies are large and in charge, rich with chocolate flavor, and the perfect combination of chewy, firm around the outside, yet soft in the center. These are the cookies you make when you want to impress someone!*

Photo Credit: Kelly Peloza

½ cup chocolate chips (for melting)

½ cup soy milk

⅔ cup canola oil

2 teaspoons vanilla

1 ⅓ cups sugar

2 tablespoons cornstarch

2 cups flour

⅔ cup cocoa

2 teaspoons baking powder

¼ teaspoon salt

⅔ cup chocolate chips

Preheat oven to 350°F. Melt the chocolate chips with ⅓ cup of the soy milk in either a microwave or in a glass dish placed in a saucepan of boiling water (makeshift double-boiler). Pour the melted chocolate and soy milk into a large bowl, then add the rest of the soy milk, oil, vanilla, sugar, and cornstarch. Add in the flour (unsifted), cocoa, baking powder, and salt. Stir until thoroughly mixed, and then add the chocolate chips.

Here comes the super-fun part! Using your hands (or, if you must, a spoon—but I suggest you live a little, and dig in to the most chocolate-y cookie dough ever!), grab handfuls of cookie dough and flatten them out to a little thicker than ½ inch on a cookie sheet lined with parchment paper. Bake for about 15 minutes (less time for smaller cookies), or until the edges are very firm and the centers look chewy and are soft to the touch.

Let them rest on the cookie sheet for a minute or so, then very carefully transfer to the cooling rack. Eat them warm if you can't resist, but they're great at room temperature as well.

Variations:

- Replace ¼ teaspoon of the vanilla with almond extract.
- Replace 1 teaspoon of the vanilla with a fruit extract, such as raspberry or strawberry.
- Add ½ teaspoon cinnamon to the dough.
- Add 1 teaspoon ground coffee beans, or replace 1 teaspoon of the vanilla with coffee extract.
- Add 2 teaspoons of orange zest for chocolate-orange cookies.

LADYBROS APPLE PIE BY SUGAR BEAT SWEETS

Yields one 9-inch pie.

Classic apple pie in a flaky crust; what could be better? This recipe comes from Sugar Beat Sweets, the bakery I own with my ladybros in San Francisco. This was developed when we expanded from our signature cupcakes to a full line of tasty pastries. The filling gets a boost in flavor from apple jelly and apple cider, which makes this intensely apple-flavored and super-delicious. A food processor makes for easy piecrust, but if you don't have one, it can be done with a pastry cutter or a fork. Although this is a little bit more involved than your typical apple pie recipe, the extra steps make all the difference!

Double Piecrust:

1 cup all-purpose flour

⅔ cup pastry flour

½ teaspoon salt

1 tablespoon sugar

1½ ounces Earth Balance or other vegan margarine

2 ounces vegetable shortening

¼ cup cold water

Photo Credit: Nicole Carpenter

Filling:

3 to 3 ½ pounds of apples (use a mixture of whatever's flavorful and local), about 6 large apples, cut into ½-inch pieces

½ cup sugar (use brown sugar for a more caramel-like pie filling)

3 tablespoons tapioca starch

2 tablespoons apple jelly

1 tablespoon apple cider

2 teaspoons freshly squeezed lemon or lime juice

¼ teaspoon salt

1 teaspoon cinnamon

Place all of the crust ingredients in the fridge or freezer before making the dough. Don't skip this step, as it helps you attain that perfect flaky crust! Once all the ingredients are chilled, pulse the dry ingredients together in a food processor for 10 seconds until combined. Add the Earth Balance and shortening, and pulse again until the mixture resembles small crumbs. Next, slowly drizzle cold water over the mixture and pulse in the food processor, just until dough begins to form; it shouldn't take the full ¼ cup. You should be able to pinch the dough and have it hold together.

Separate the dough into two parts and flatten each half into ½-inch discs. Wrap the discs in aluminum foil or plastic wrap and refrigerate for at least 1 hour (and up to 24 hours) before rolling out.

Filling:

Peel and slice the apples into ½-inch slices. Next, place the apple slices into a large bowl and mix with ¼ cup of the sugar, making sure that you get sugar on each apple slice. Place the sugared apple slices in a large colander over the bowl you used to mix

Marika

Location: Toronto, Canada

Blog: Madcap Cupcake (madcapcupcake.wordpress.com)

Reason I Went Vegan: A few years ago I witnessed an incident on the local news about a truck transporting cattle to slaughter that had overturned on the highway. Four steer escaped and ran terrified through a nearby residential neighborhood. Officials rounded up all but one of the steer on the loose. When that fourth terrified steer knocked down a news camera on someone's driveway, police opted to shoot him. As they opened fire and a hail of bullets started to hit the frightened animal, he looked back at the police with a confused expression on his face before he finally, and slowly, went down. I'd been vegetarian for seven years prior, but in that moment, I knew instantly that I would never participate in the exploitation of animals in any way, shape, or form, ever again. I didn't want him to die in vain. I've been vegan ever since.

Favorite Dish to Cook: When it's just us, you can't beat sourdough pizza with mushrooms, kale, and tofu ricotta; and if I'm trying to impress guests, I love organic spelt penne with wilted baby spinach and almond ricotta; it's so simple and elegant.

Favorite "Accidentally Vegan" Treat: It's a toss-up between Christie's Pirate Cookies and Ritter Sport's Dark Chocolate Marzipan.

the apple slices and sugar. Leave the sugared apple slices for 90 minutes. When you come back, you should find that the apples have released some of their liquid into the bowl.

When you're ready to bake, preheat the oven to 425°F. Roll one disc of dough out thinly on a well-floured surface. Gently place the dough into a 9-inch pie plate and carefully press it in. Next, trim the excess dough from around the edges of the pie plate, and you're ready to fill.

Add the rest of the sugar, tapioca starch, jelly, cider, lemon or lime juice, salt, and cinnamon to the bowl with the apple slices. Mix well to coat everything. Arrange the apple slices in the pie plate with your bottom piecrust. Try to get them as compact as you can; the filling will be a bit taller than the lip of the pie dish.

Roll out your second disc of dough and place it over the top of the pie. Trim the edges, and press together with the bottom crust. Cut a few diamond shapes out of the top crust to allow some of the steam to escape.

Place the pie on a cookie sheet and put it on the floor of your oven for 30 minutes. After 30 minutes, transfer it to the lower rack of the oven and bake 20 minutes more, keeping an eye on the crust. Let your pie cool for at least 30 minutes before serving.

As long as people will shed the blood of
innocent creatures there can
be no peace, no liberty, no harmony
between people. Slaughter and
justice cannot dwell together.
—Isaac Bashevis Singer

CHAPTER 7

DO IT YOURSELF!

From craft projects using recycled items to learning how to grow food in your garden, DIY is the fun and fabulous way to go! People everywhere are learning new skills and creating handmade goods to enrich their lives, to share with friends, and, in some cases, to help save the planet. Whether you're a creative rookie or a seasoned crafter, there's something fun here for everyone.

VEGAN GARDENING BY ADRIANA MARTINEZ

Adriana Martinez *is a UCCE-certified master gardener in Los Angeles County; a Community Garden manager and founder; a horticulturist, instructor, published writer, community activist, guerrilla gardener, and blogger whose uniqueness lies in blending tried-and-true gardening techniques with a punk-rock attitude. Visit her at www.anarchyinthegarden.com*

So, you want to grow a garden? Forget about green thumb vs. brown thumb—with a few pointers and a little guidance on how to cultivate and maintain your plot, you'll be ready to grow your own produce in no time. Regardless of plot size, plants need a few basic components to thrive: sunlight, soil, and water.

Veggies Need Vitamin D

Carrots aren't the only thing tomatoes love (they make great companion plants); they're also rather fond of sunlight. Plot placement is crucial: A north-south orientation is best, allowing direct sunlight to hit both sides of the bed. Most edibles require six to eight hours of full sun for maximum flavor and production. Select a leveled, sunny site that is protected from heavy wind.

From the Soil Up

Friable soil that is rich and crumbly in texture and packed with organic matter produces the best crops. If you are planting directly in the ground, determine what type of soil you'll be working with—clay, sandy, or silt.

Clay soil, referred to as heavy soil, is gritty in texture, has poor water drainage and aeration, weak root penetration, and is an overall drag to grow in. *Sandy soil* is smooth in texture and considered light. It warms up faster in spring, but water drainage and nutrient depletion also occur more quickly than in clay soil. *Silt* is somewhere between clay and sand and tends to have the characteristics of clay soil.

Loamy (friable) soil is a combo of clay (20 percent), sand (40 percent), and silt (40 percent), and is the most desirable. It contains ample organic matter, water drainage is ideal, and it expends nutrients moderately.

You can never have too much organic matter! To achieve optimal soil texture, generously fill the planting area with organic matter. Organic matter may consist of homegrown or bagged compost or green manure (cover crops). As the organic matter decays, you are rewarded with humus, the organic portion of soil resulting from partial decomposition of plant matter.

Raised Bed and Container Gardening

Where soil is inadequate or yard space is a high commodity, consider growing your plants in raised beds or containers. Organically amended and well-draining soil is readily available. Crops in raised beds produce better because the soil is deep, loose, and fertile.

Construction materials are entirely your choice: wood, redwood, or cedar (they're rot-resistant), recycled concrete, straw wattle, bricks. Be creative! I painted the exterior of my raised beds in black. However, there is one rule of thumb when constructing your raised beds: Keep them narrow, no wider than 4 feet. This width will facilitate easy reach to the center of the bed, eliminating the need to step inside and compact the soil.

Watering

Sufficient water is essential for plant growth. Concerns over water conservation and water restrictions have led to a reevaluation of watering practices. Despite these constraints, a bountiful garden is possible.

Factors like soil texture, plant maturity, and weather determine the frequency and amount of water a garden will require. Water absorption is essential to seed germination. For seeds and seedlings, keep the soil moist, but not soggy. As immature plants begin to grow and roots stretch deeper, scale back your watering. Established plants require deep, occasional watering, about 1 inch of water per week. Deep watering encourages deep rooting, which leads to stronger, healthier plants. One inch of water will penetrate sandy soil about 12 inches; loam, about 7 inches; and clay soils, 5 inches or less. Avoid shallow, frequent watering, as this will lead to shallow root systems and high water loss through evaporation.

Test soil moisture before watering. Insert your finger or trowel 3 inches into the soil. If it feels dry, it's time to water. Water slowly and for a long time, so the moisture sinks deeply into the ground. To check water penetration, water for a set amount of time (say, fifteen minutes). Wait for twenty-four hours, then use a soil-sampling tube or dig a hole to check for moisture. You'll soon learn to judge how long to water each plant in order to thoroughly soak its root zone.

The best time to water is in the early morning, before temperatures begin to rise. This gives the plants a good supply of water to face the heat of the day, and it reduces evaporation. Late-afternoon watering is also acceptable; however, watering should take place early enough so that the plants' leaves have enough time to dry before nightfall (wet leaves at night can cause the development of fungal diseases). Choose a watering method that will not wet the leaves, like drip irrigation or water at the base. Don't forget the mulch, as it slows evaporation and is essential to water conservation.

Seeds vs. Vegetable Starts

Growing from seed is one of the most rewarding facets of gardening, but careful planning is required. Don't fret if you missed your seed-starting date for some crops. Your local independent nursery will carry a variety of vegetables suitable for growing in your area. Although they will be higher-priced than a packet of seeds, you will be assured a harvest.

Starting seeds indoors not only gives you a jump-start on the season—especially if you live in a cooler climate—but the available seed variety is also unparalleled. Spring seed sowing requires knowing the previous year's last frost date (or the average of the past few years) in your area. Once you have identified your frost date, count back the number of weeks indicated on the seed packet to determine the appropriate seed-starting date. Keeping a seed-starting journal is imperative!

Vegan Fertilizers and Healthy Soil

Now that you've got the basics of organic gardening down, extending your herbivore kick-ass way of living to your veggie plot is easy. Soil fertility and ideal soil

Jeanette Zeis

Business Name: Jeanette Zeis Ceramics / VeganDish
Web Site / Location: www.jeanettezeis.com; www.vegandish.net;
Atlanta, Georgia

What motivated you to start your business?

Dissatisfaction can be a big motivator. I had been working with clay for several years and hadn't really thought about selling my pottery, but then I came to the conclusion that I didn't want to work for other people the rest of my life. So, I had to find a way to make a living, and since my only real skill is making pottery, that's the route I took. Plus, I couldn't think of any better way to spend the day than elbow-deep in clay.

Do you put an emphasis on the vegan aspect of the company, and, if so, do you find that it works in your favor?

I have a full line of pottery that is made for vegans. It is a substantial part of my company, and I am very proud of it. I have found it beneficial to keep my veganism at the forefront. People will ask me questions

about being vegan, or they are excited to come across a fellow vegan. It is such an important part of who I am, and I think people respond to learning something personal about the businesses they choose to support.

What's the most rewarding part of running a vegan business?

Running my own vegan business allows me to make a living without having to compromise my beliefs. Plus, I have met some amazing vegans from all over the world.

What's your favorite item that you sell?

Probably the vegan mugs. I love the idea that people might take their mugs to the office, and it might start a conversation about being vegan. Or the large serving bowls, because I know they are going to be filled with something delicious that will be enjoyed by other vegans (as well as non-vegans).

composition are maintained by crop rotation, and utilizing compost and fertilizers that are free of animal by-products. Simply put, vegan organic gardening, or "veganic gardening," is a method of cultivating crops without the use of petro-based chemicals, stock manures, or animal by-products, such as blood meal, bone meal, fish meal, or anything from animal origin.

Crop rotation involves planting in different locations from one year to the next. Rotating your crops reduces the depletion of soil nutrients and curtails the buildup of pathogens and pests. If you are planting in containers, the soil should be replaced with each new planting.

Compost is a gardener's best friend. It can be used as a soil amendment or top dressing for plants. This rich, crumbly loam is produced by combining equal amounts of brown matter (carbon)—dried leaves, straw, and paper shreds—with green matter (nitrogen), including grass clippings, kitchen scraps, and coffee grounds. You will water, turn, and wait, and depending on the amount of material that is added, garden-ready compost should be ready in about four to six weeks.

The thought of bone and blood meal make me gag. There are several *fertilizers* free of these by-products. Here are some alternatives:

Alfalfa meal: Used in place of blood meal; good source of nitrogen, balanced with phosphorus and potassium. Roses and flowering shrubs love alfalfa!

Seaweed: Loaded with trace elements that are essential to a plant's growth and survival. Seaweed makes an excellent foliar fertilizer.

Neem meal: Derived from the neem tree, this fertilizer enhances plant immunity, encourages top growth and bud set, and strengthens roots.

Vegan organic gardening is compassionate agriculture. Gardens, like people, flourish sans animal products. Go forth and grow veganically!

POTTY POTS BY ADRIANA MARTINEZ

We all use it, often purchasing it in bulk, discreetly reaching for a twelve-pack. The mystery item? *Toilet paper.* Once it's used up, we're left with a pliable cardboard tube. Instead of tossing these in the trash bin, you can "up-cycle" the tubular remains into a seed-starting container. Potty Pots are awesome on many levels. Not only do they provide their own carbon (cardboard equals brown matter), an essential ingredient in compost, but by using them for gardening, we decrease the landfill's load—and the built-in collar keeps the cutworm at bay. Score!

Fill the tubes with your favorite soil-less seed-starting mix, or make your own (see recipe below), and let the seeding begin!

Materials Needed

Toilet paper tube

Scissors

Instructions

Flatten the tube and smooth out the edges, creating two sharp creases. Open the rectangular cardboard and flatten the tube again, creasing it and creating four sharp edges. You are ultimately fashioning a square out of the toilet paper roll. Cut 1 ½-inch slits on all four sides and fold in. Then, unfold the sides, alternating one by one, to create a sturdy bottom.

Peat-Free Seed-Starting Mix

1 part coconut coir

1 part perlite (improves drainage)

1 part finely sifted compost or worm castings (enhances aeration and water retention)

Once the second set of leaves emerge, water your seedlings with a mild fertilizer (i.e., one derived from kelp).

DIY DESSERT STANDS

Handmade stands to display desserts are easy to make, not to mention adorable when adorned with cupcakes, cookies, or other sweets. These stands are also eco-friendly, as they're a great way to recycle old plates or use "thrift scores" to make something fun. I love searching for the perfect combinations at secondhand shops, and I have used these stands everywhere from craft fairs to bake sales!

Items Needed

Sturdy plates, ideally vintage or secondhand

Vases or candlestick holders with heavy bases and a flat surface on top

Strong epoxy

Measuring tape

A pencil

Start by cleaning all of your pieces and making sure they're completely dry before proceeding. Plan which items you'll be matching together in advance, making sure they can balance on their own, or they won't balance after they are glued together. Measure and mark the center of your plates with a pencil, then lay out the plates with the marked backside showing in an area where they can stay to dry.

On a disposable surface, mix your epoxy according to the manufacturer's instructions, and then apply it to the top portion of the base. Allow the epoxy to set for a few minutes, and then press the base firmly onto the plate. Scrape the excess epoxy off, making sure not to get it on your fingers.

Let the stands dry untouched overnight. Meanwhile, bake some sweets to display!

HOW TO FROST A CUPCAKE

It's always fun when cupcakes dress to impress with fluffy frosting piped high, but whether that's a reality for your sweet treats depends on you and your frosting skills. If you want to take a break from plopping frosting on top of your cupcakes with a knife, and really impress your friends with some bakery-style swirls, keep reading!

Frosting 3

Photo Credit: Patrick Rafanan

Besides your cupcakes and a bowl of frosting, you'll need a pastry bag and a piping tip. A reusable pastry bag is a great investment; it's more eco-friendly than disposable ones, and it's also sturdier.

The piping tip you use is very important. Ideally, you should have a large, open star tip, like an Ateco 825 or a Magic Tip 5ST. At your local craft store, you may find a Wilton 1M, which is fine for mini cupcakes or cake borders, but you really need to bring out the big guns here, so head to a bakery supply shop, or order one online.

Start with a clean cupcake and a filled pastry bag with the top twisted closed and no air bubbles inside. Holding the bag directly over the cupcake, in a quick, continuous motion, make a circle just short of the outer edge of the cupcake, then continue to spiral, making a smaller circle on top of that, slightly overlapping on the first circle, and then a final small swirl to fill in the remaining space. You should end in the very middle of the cupcake. When you reach the middle, lift up the bag, allowing a peak to form on top. The key is consistent pressure, allowing an even amount of frosting to flow from the bag. Practice makes perfect, so don't be afraid to have a practice cupcake to frost and re-frost until you get the look you desire!

REUSABLE PRODUCE BAGS BY ERIKA LARSON

Erika Larson is one crafty bitch, from reusable feminine products to etched glass, her Etsy shop Strange and Violent Creations (www.etsy.com/shop/strangeandviolent) has everything for the modern woman. In a world where eco-friendly bags are pushed on us, only to be made of polypropylene, the same crap as plastic bags, we need to wise up and be truly green. Erika is hooking you up with a fun and adorable way to reduce waste and get your craft on!

It used to be that only the dreadlocked earth mama walking around barefoot in front of the granola display would bring her own shopping bags to the store. The checker and/or bagger would give her a puzzled look and cautiously peep into the empty bags as if they half-expected to find cat vomit inside them. Then they would still double-bag the jug of orange juice—you know, the one with a handle—in a swaddling of protective petroleum-based plastic.

Now everyone and their grandma have reusable shopping bags! The bags range from canvas cotton totes to those little square green ones made of recycled plastic bottles, store merchandise to branded promos, and even those designer I'M NOT A PLASTIC BAG bags that everyone went nuts for a few years ago. The best part is that you don't get the weird looks from the bagger anymore.

There's still one area in the store where even the most well-meaning environmentalist can wreak some major havoc, however, and that is the produce section. Huge rolls of plastic bags lay in wait to transport your carrots home, where they'll get promptly tossed away. I used to try and rinse out the plastic bags, but seriously—have you ever tried that? The bags get gross and they take forever to dry. With reusable fabric produce bags running at $5 a pop, here's a quick and easy way to make your own at home. You'll be saving some green, in more ways than one.

Materials

Pick your fabric and cording; ideally, you'll want a thin cotton muslin, faille, or netting. Don't feel hemmed in by these options, but keep in mind what you'll be putting in your bags (big apples or teeny little flaxseeds?), and that you will want to easily machine-wash and dry your bags. A yard of fabric is a good place to start; it will yield a couple of good-size produce bags for you to try out. Consider prewashing the fabric in order to get any shrinkage out of the way before you cut and sew. Feel free to decorate your fabric using stencils or stamps with fabric paint.

You want a durable but soft and flexible cording for the bag's drawstrings. Eighth-inch diameter cording is ideal, but you can get larger or smaller depending on the size of the bags you are making. To estimate how much cording you will need for each bag, double the circumference of the bag opening and add 6 inches.

Measure and Cut

Measure and cut the size bag you want. These bags are so easy that we're not even including a pattern here; just make sure the width of your bag is at a 1:3 ratio to the length of your bag. For example, if you want to make a produce bag, cut a rectangle approximately 10 inches wide and 30 inches long. You would probably want to cut a smaller spice bag 4 inches by 12 inches. Be sure to cut the length along the grain of the fabric (see page 203).

Sew the Casing

Sew the casing for the drawstrings. Measure down 1 ¼ inches from the top of the bag and cut a ¼-inch-deep notch parallel to the top. Fold the fabric above the notch ⅛ inch, and then once again, toward the inside center of the bag. Stitch the folded edge in place. This should give you a nice clean edge where the drawstring will come out, and will not fray the fabric through repeated use. Repeat this process with the

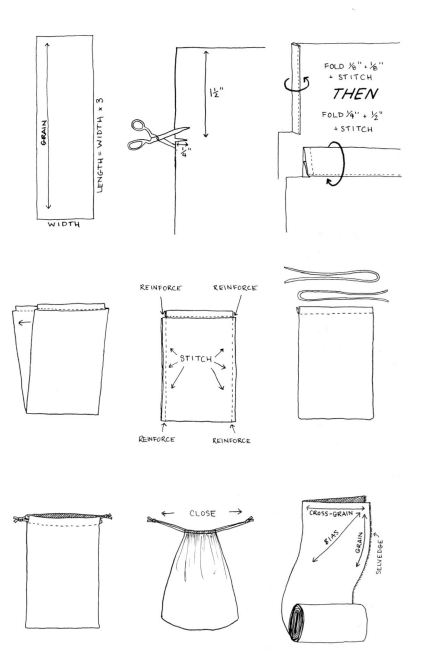

remaining three corners of the bag, taking care to ensure that the folded edges are on the inside of the bag.

Once you have finished the edges of the drawstring casings, fold the top edge of the bag toward the inside center ¼ inch, then once again at ½ inch. The resulting edge should meet, but not overlap, the top of the notch cut along the side of the bag. Stitch this folded edge in place. You should now have a tube through which you will soon insert the drawstrings.

Sew the Sides

Fold the bag in half, inside out, across the length, so that the drawstring casings on either side meet each other. You will want to stitch along the sides of the bag from the notch to the fold at the bottom, ¼ inch away from the edge. Double-stitch or back-tack at the notch and the fold, where the most pressure will be on the bag, to prevent the bag from tearing or leaking. To extend the life of the bag, you will want to finish the inside seams to prevent or slow the fraying process. If you're lucky enough to have a serger or marrow machine, finish the edges that way. If not, you can use a zigzag stitch along the raw edge of the seam, or even trim the raw edge with pinking shears.

Thread the Drawstring

Flip the bag right side out and cut your drawstring pieces. You want two equal lengths of cording, each the length of the bag opening circumference, plus about 3 inches. Feel free to cut more generously if you need to. Wrap the raw edge of the cord with tape to more easily thread it through the casing, and then feed the cord through the casings, knotting it together where the raw edges meet at one side. Repeat with the other length of cord, knotting the raw edges on the opposite side of the first knot. Trim the extra cord coming out of the knots with scissors. If the cording is poly or nylon, you can singe the edges with a lighter or match to create a bead and prevent fraying. To close the bag, simply pull the knots in opposite directions.

Go Shopping!

Your new produce bags should hardly register on a commercial scale, so your produce won't cost any more than it usually does. If they get stained or messy, you can just pop them in the machine with your next load of laundry. Remember that these aren't airtight, so if you buy cereal or crunchy snacks, you will want to transfer them to airtight containers when you get home.

Woven fabric is made up of yarns that have been combined together. The yarn that is threaded through the loom is called the *warp;* the yarn that is threaded through the warp to make fabric is called the *weft.* In a finished piece of fabric, this is called the *grain* and the *cross-grain.* The grain is the direction in a piece of woven fabric that has the least amount of stretch, so knowing where on the grain to cut a pattern is very important when it comes to how to the finished piece will behave and wear. In this pattern you want to cut "on the grain," meaning that the length of the bag will be parallel to the grain. The grain always runs parallel to the length edge of a piece of fabric, called the *selvedge.* With this pattern, just cut the length of the bag in the same direction as the length of your fabric.

RECIPE CARDS

Whether it's a family recipe that's been passed down through the years, or your favorite recipe from a book that you're passing on to a vegan-curious friend, the recipe cards on page 204 will come in handy, and they're mighty cute too! Illustrator Michelle Cavigliano, from MyZoetrope.com, and the artist behind the drawings you've seen in this book, created these after I mentioned how much I love the ones in her Etsy shop.

To print: Photocopy this page onto a lightweight piece of paper, then photocopy that page onto heavy cardstock. Cut out and enjoy!

CROSS-STITCH BASICS BY CITY DOWN

Counted cross stitch is easy and fun! You are simply transferring a design from a printed graph onto cross-stitch fabric, called Aida. The stitcher uses embroidery floss to stitch an X made up of two diagonal stitches, which, put together, form the X. It's simple to follow the pattern, stitching the Xs on the fabric that correspond to the symbols on the chart. Each colored square on the chart represents one X on the fabric. The different colors on the chart represent the different colors of floss. When you see simple lines on a pattern, these represent the backstitch, which is just stitching a line following the lines on the pattern.

A Bit about Floss

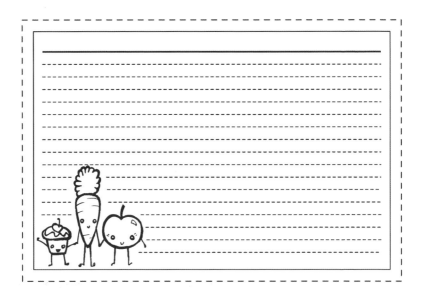

Embroidery floss is a cotton thread used for stitching which comes in a skein and has six strands. For cross stitch, we use only two strands at a time for stitching.

For backstitching, usually only one thread is used, but I have made the choice to use two strands to make the backstitched facial features on your zombie stand out.

To separate your two strands from the thread, hold one end of the length between two fingers, then select two strands and slowly pull them out.

Before you jump right in and get stitching, it's important to read these instructions completely. You don't want to miss anything important!

Cross-Stitch Supplies

For this project you will need the following:

Fabric: 14-count Aida cross-stitch fabric, 9 inches wide x 7 inches

Graph: This is the Stitch'd Ink pattern included in this rad book, and the design you will be working from.

Needle: Size 24 tapestry needle.

DMC embroidery floss: 666, 726, 164, 996, 310 (or feel free to use your own choice of colors).

Scissors: You can use any pair of scissors, but a nice pair of small embroidery scissors will make your job easier.

Embroidery hoop: For beginners, a plastic or wooden embroidery hoop is helpful to hold the fabric taut while you stitch, but you can stitch without one.

Let's Get Started

To get started stitching, first, grab your Aida fabric and find the center. An easy way to do this is to fold the fabric in half and then in half again, and then press with your hand. Using the crease in the center you may find it helpful to place a pin through this point so you don't lose it! Most stitchers like to start stitching close to the center of the design. The design you're stitching is landscape (horizontal), so make sure you have your fabric laid out horizontally.

Next, find the center of the graph. This is where the red horizontal and vertical lines on the pattern intersect. You may start stitching on the center square, or you can count up or out to an outside square.

Grab a piece of thread in the color you are going to start stitching with. Cut a length approximately 20 inches (50 cm) in length.

Tracy Perkins

Business Name: Strawberry Hedgehog
Web Site: http://strawberryhedgehog.com

Do you put an emphasis on the vegan aspect of the company, and, if so, do you find that it works in your favor?

I feel like I am making the vegan aspect of my company clear, even if many don't understand or care. I put it on my signs and use it as part of how I describe my business, on business cards, signs, etcetra. I know a majority of my customers are not vegan, but those who are have a stronger dedication and loyalty to my brand. I love to feel like I am making it easier for them to find what they need, and to treat themselves well without the hassle of having to read the labels every time. That's because all of it is vegan, and all of it is fabulous!

How do you handle any animosity toward veganism in your personal life or business?

I usually joke around with people who are hostile toward my choice to be vegan. That is not to say I don't have serious conversations about it, but I think keeping things light, factual, and nonjudgmental is important. As soon as you start to act defensive or hostile in response, no one will hear what you're saying. It's always best to try to take the high road, and why not have a laugh while you're there?

What's your favorite item that you sell?

I love all of my products, but my soaps in particular are my favorite. They are like my babies! Every month I get to dream up new scents for my Soap of the Month Club, and come up with new designs, etcetra. It is the highlight of my business, and I know my customers love the variety, too.

Favorite vegan meal (to cook or when dining out)?

I love eating and cooking, so it's nearly impossible to narrow it down. My favorite meal to make is just a simple stir-fry with a spicy peanut sauce over rice noodles. It is so versatile, colorful, and simple. You can't beat a great vegan cupcake, either.

strawberryhedgehog.com

First method diagram

Up at A, down at B, up at C, down at B, up at D, down at C, up at E, down at D, up at F, down at E.

Second method diagram

Back stitch diagram

Do not use any knots to start or end, as these knots on the back will show through. To begin stitching, bring the threaded needle up from the back of the fabric, leaving about a 1-inch (2.5-cm) tail of thread behind the fabric. Stitch the next five or six stitches over the tail. Clip off extra thread.

When you need to move from one area to another using the same-color thread, don't carry your thread for more than 1 inch (2.5 cm) across the back of the fabric, because the strands will show through the fabric holes. It's much better to end in one area and then start again in another.

When it's time to end with one piece of thread, turn your design over and weave your needle back through the last five or six stitches and clip off any extra thread.

Stitching Time

There are two methods of creating your stitches. The first is to work a row of half stitches (/////), and then to work back (\\\\\) to complete the Xs. This is the method you will use for most stitching, and it can save a lot of time. The second method is to complete each X as you go. This method is best used for vertical rows of stitches. It is important that all your Xs are crossed in the same direction. This means the top thread of the X should always slant in the same direction (\), running from the upper-left corner to the bottom-right corner. If the Xs are mixed, the finished piece will look uneven, and we want your finished cross stitch looking fabulous! If the strands become twisted as you stitch, simply drop the threaded needle and let it dangle from the fabric. The strands will unwind.

Try to relax as you stitch. Once you get the hang of it, you will find that you get into a rhythm and start to enjoy the process. Your stitches should lie flat on your fabric and not distort the holes or the fabric, so try to keep your tension even.

Backstitching

Backstitching is a running stitch (not an X) used to outline an area or to form lettering. Normally you would use one less strand of floss for backstitching than you used for cross stitching, but I have made the choice to use two strands for backstitching in this project.

Finishing

When your stitching is complete, it's a good idea to finish your piece. After all, you've put a lot of hard work into this beautiful cross stitch. Simply wash in cool water using a mild liquid detergent. Rinse well. Do not wring, but roll in a clean towel to absorb most of the water. While still damp, place face down on a terry-cloth towel. Place another cloth on top of the needlework and press lightly with a warm iron. Let dry, then frame and admire your amazing skills!

- DMC 666
- DMC 726
- DMC 164
- DMC 996
- DMC 310

RECYCLED GIFT BOWS

There's a lot of waste in this world, especially when it comes to paper products. Junk mail clogs our mailboxes and old magazines and newspapers litter our houses, making it easy to fill a recycling bin in no time. One way to use the excess paper in your life is not only to wrap presents in boxes covered by the funny pages, but also to top them with a homemade recycled gift bow!

This is a fun and easy project that may seem tricky at first, but once you get the hang of it, you can make them in no time! I like to use issues of *Martha Stewart Living* for the amazing colors on the pages, but anything will do.

Items Needed

- A page from a magazine or a piece of junk mail (the more colorful, the better!)
- Scissors
- Tape and a stapler, or a brass paper fastener (brad)

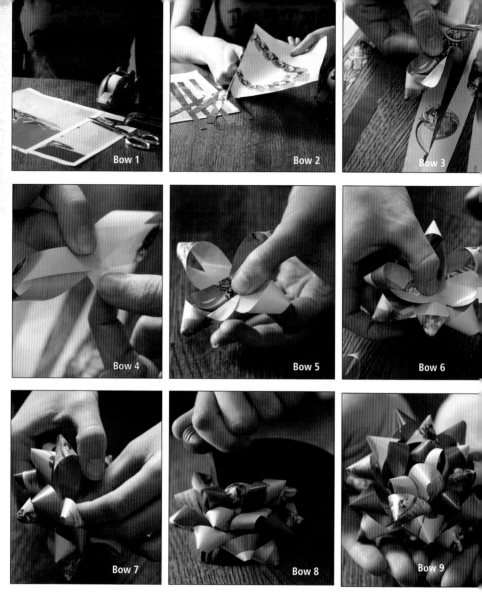

Cut your page vertically in strips of equal width, at least ¾-inch wide, forming at least nine strips. The thinner your strips are, the more you will need.

Holding your strip in the center in one hand, with the less-colorful side face up, form a coned loop with the part of the page above your finger and another loop the opposite way with the bottom of the page. You should have formed a figure-eight shape, with the page ends overlapping on the back.

For a non-twisted loop bow, hold the strip in the center with the less-colorful side face up, and then form two loops by bringing each end to the center, slightly overlapping.

If you're using a tape and stapler method, put a tiny piece of tape where the ends meet in the back and move on to your next strip.Once all of your loops are formed, layer them on top of each other, making sure each layer is pointing a different direction than the last, until you have a full bow going all the way up and filling in the center. Use a staple in the center to attach all of the layers together, and then arrange the bow loops to be full and fluffy.

If you're using the brad method, push the point through the middle of the loop and move on to your next strip. You can add each strip as you go, making sure to change the direction of the bow points for each layer; or, you can make the layers of the bow, arrange it, and then add the fastener at the end.

KNITTING WITH VEGAN FIBERS BY KRISTEN BLACKMORE

Going into a yarn shop as a new vegan, a knitter, or both, can be downright intimidating, but it doesn't have to be. Yes, these stores make most of their profit by selling animal fibers, and the staff doesn't always know how to handle people who don't want to use these products—but if you walk in prepared with knowledge of the yarns and fibers that will work well for your particular project, you can still have a great experience. Just try not to fight with the employees if they corner you to lecture about how you're missing out on the "best" yarns (it's happened before). This handy guide to vegan fibers and yarns will help you navigate your way through the shelves and guarantee that your crafts are not only cute, but free of animal exploitation.

Springtime Cardigans, Pullovers, and Tank Tops

With some careful attention to finding the right gauge, sweaters can be knit out of almost any weight of yarn on any needle size. Cotton is a fantastic fiber for sweaters but often gets overlooked by the wool-obsessed knitting world. Lighter cardigans, pullovers, and especially anything with lace detail tend to look great when knit with cotton. Cotton does have a tendency to stretch and grow with wear, but luckily it can be machine-washed and shrunk back to its original size after a spin in the dryer.

While plant fibers inherently have a smaller ecological footprint than animal fibers, sourcing organic yarns will further limit your impact on the planet. Cotton production is responsible for 25 percent of U.S. pesticide use, but choosing one of the many organic cotton yarns nullifies your contribution to the problem. Larger yarn companies such as Lion Brand, Bernat, and Knit Picks all make inexpensive and commonly available organic cotton, while Blue Sky Alpacas sells a pricier, more luxurious organic cotton.

Besides cotton, you may also encounter fibers like linen, hemp, bamboo, and soy. On their own or as a blend, they all make great short-sleeved knits for warm weather because of their breathability. For example, Crystal Palace Bamboozle (bamboo/cotton/nylon) would be a great yarn for a summery sweater, as the extra nylon would keep the garment from stretching and growing.

Winter Sweaters

If you're looking to make a sweater that's suitable for snowy winters, plant-based yarns might not fit the bill. That's where acrylic comes in.

Acrylic is a synthetic fiber invented to be a cheap alternative to wool. Some knitters see acrylic as the root of all evil, but try viewing it more as a bad habit—sometimes you just need winter insulation. Being a petroleum product, you can't pretend it's great for the planet, but then again, neither is the wool industry. That said, do stay away from yarn that is more than 50 percent acrylic because it can start to feel like you're knitting with plastic.

Rowan Calmer, a 75 percent cotton and 25 percent acrylic, makes a really cozy sweater, and Berroco Comfort, a 50/50 acrylic/nylon blend, is quite soft and holds its shape extremely well. Even the names of these yarns sound warm and snuggly!

Environmentally savvy crafters can search for acrylic sweaters at local thrift stores to reclaim and repurpose the yarn for their own projects. Check the tags on the sweaters to find the perfect fiber content and then rip away. When choosing a sweater, make sure to take into account any sagginess or pilling—you don't want to knit with bad yarn!

Socks

When you set out to make a pair of socks, first decide whether you want warm or light socks. Bamboo is the best natural choice for warm winter socks, but interestingly, the fiber will also keep you cool in the summer. An acrylic/nylon blend such as Berroco Comfort Sock yarn will also get the job done. If you don't care about warmth, then have a blast and pick out any fiber you want.

Look for yarns with a bit of nylon, because without it, the socks will end up baggy and fall down around your ankles after just a few wears. Remember that not all synthetic fibers come with a stretch; stick with nylon or elastic, as anything else will leave you with nothing but big ol' Christmas stockings.

If you want to make socks thin enough to wear with your normal-size shoe, seek out fingering weight yarn. Bernat, Cascade, Crystal Palace, Elann, Kollage, and Kraemer all make great plant-based fingering weight yarns from fibers like corn, soy, bamboo, and cotton.

Mittens and Gloves

Hands are pretty much feet with thumbs, so you'll want the same type of elasticity for mittens and gloves as you would for socks. Seeing as you won't be putting shoes over your mittens, you get more wiggle room when choosing the yarn weight.

Bamboozle, as mentioned in the sweater section, is an aran-weight yarn, which would also work perfectly for mittens. Wick, produced by Knit One, Crochet Too, is a really neat worsted-weight yarn made from soy with some added polypropylene, a synthetic that attracts moisture. This helps if wearing mittens in the winter causes your palms to begin sweating profusely (it happens—don't judge). You can also try any of the yarns suitable for making warm sweaters or socks.

As for scarves, hats, and everything else, go crazy and experiment with yarns of different weight and texture. Knitting can be very much a trial-and-error process, so start with small projects and figure out the yarns and fibers you like before jumping into your first sweater. If you're poking around a yarn shop and find a skein of something you're attracted to, buy it, swatch it, and it will tell you what it wants to be. Before you know it you'll be on your way to knitting just about anything you want, sans cruelty.

KNIT HEADBAND BY KRISTEN BLACKMORE

This adorable headband is a fun project that only takes a couple of hours to complete. If you have some basic knitting skills, you should be able to hook yourself up with a new stylish accessory and be the envy of your friends!

Supplies
(MC) 1 ball of Berroco Comfort DK in black
(CC) 1 ball of Berroco Comfort DK in pink
Size 5 knitting needles

Size F crochet hook

Tapestry needle

Gauge

22 sts and 36 rows over 4 inches on size 5 needles

Abbreviations

CO: cast on

sts: stitches

Sl1: slip one

k: knit

p: purl

WS: wrong side

YO: yarn over

K2tog: knit two together

K3tog: knit three together

K4tog: Knit four together

psso: pass the slipped stitch over the knit stitch

BO: bind off

Photo Credit: Jeanine Michelle

Skills required

Cast on, knitting, purling, increasing, decreasing, i-cord, crochet crab stitch, binding off, weaving in ends.

Note: Be sure and slip the first stitch of every row on the body of the headband so that you can crochet the border later.

Instructions

With MC CO 6 sts

Row 1: Sl1, knit to the end of row.

Row 2: Sl1, purl to the end of row.

Repeat rows 1 & 2 twenty more times, ending on the ws.

Begin increasing:

Row 23: sl1, k1, yo, k2, yo, k2 (8 sts).

Row 24–26: Work in stockinette beginning with a purl row.

Row 27: sl1, k1, yo, k2tog, ssk, yo, k2 (8 sts).

Row 28–30: Work in stockinette.

Row 31: sl1, k1, yo, knit to last 2 sts, yo, k2.

Row 32–34: Work in stockinette.

Row 35: sl1, k1, yo, k2tog, knit to last 4 sts, ssk, yo, k2 (10 sts).

Row 36–38: Work in stockinette.

Repeat rows 31–38, three times (18 sts on needle).

Row 62: sl1, k1, yo, knit to last 2 sts, yo, k2.

Row 63–65: Work in stockinette.

Top of the headband:

Row 66: Sl1, k1, yo, k2tog, knit to last 4 sts, ssk, yo, k2.

Row 67–69: Work in stockinette.

Repeat row 66–69, twice.

Begin decreasing:

Row 77: Sl1, k1, yo, k3tog, knit to last 5 sts, sl1, k2tog, psso, yo, k2.

Row 78–80: Work in stockinette.

Row 81: S11, k1, yo, k2tog, knit to last 4 sts, ssk, yo, k2.

Row 82–84: Work in stockinette.

Repeat rows 77–84, four times.

Row 116: Sl1, k1, yo, k4tog, yo, k2.

Row 117: Sl1, purl.

Row 118: sl1, k1, k2tog, ssk, k2 (6 sts remain on needle).

Work 22 rows in stockinette, slipping the first stitch of every row.

BO all sts.

Crochet the border: With size F crochet hook and CC, crab-stitch on both edges of the headband.

Make bow:

Body: With CC CO 22 sts, work 14 rows in stockinette stitch. BO all sts.

Center tie: With CC CO 3 sts and work 7 rows in stockinette using i-cord. BO all sts.

Wrap the center tie tightly around the center of the bow body and secure.

Finishing:

Stitch the bottom edge of the headband together.

Attach the bow to the headband about 6 inches above the center back seam.

Weave in loose ends, and then try it on! Don't you look cute!

KNIT CUPCAKE POTHOLDER BY HANNAH KAMINSKY

Knitters, grab your needles and some yarn so you can make the cutest potholder you ever did see! Hannah Kaminsky, author of *My Sweet Vegan* and the Bittersweet blog, is a dynamo not only in the kitchen, but also when it comes to all things crafty!

Photo Credit: Hannah Kaminsky

She whipped up this adorable knitting pattern, so when you're done making these, you can use them to remove her Purple Cow Cupcakes (recipe on page 175) from the oven!

Cake (make 4)

With brown or tan worsted-weight cotton yarn, ch 25

Row 1: (WS) dc in second ch from hook, dc in next 4 chs, sc in remaining chs. Ch1, turn (24 sc)

Row 2: (RS) sc in each st across. Ch1, turn.

Row 3: Working in back loops only, dc in next 5 sts, sc in remaining sts. Ch1, turn

Rows 4–27: repeat rows 2 and 3.

Tie off.

Frosting

Row 1: With frosting color and RS facing, attach yarn with a sc to the widest edge—right corner. Evenly space 34 sc total along the top edge. Ch1, turn. (34)

Row 2: Sc twice into one st, sc until the last st, sc twice into one. Ch1, turn. (36)

Row 3: Sc twice into one st, sc until the last st, sc twice into one. Ch1, turn. (38)

Row 4: Sc twice into one st, sc until the last st, sc twice into one. Ch1, turn. (40)

Rows 5–8: Sc across. Ch1, turn.

Row 9: Sc2tog twice, sc until the last 4 sts, sc2tog twice. Ch1, turn. (36)

Row 10: Sc2tog, sc until last 2 sts, sc2tog. Ch1, turn. (34)

Rows 11 and 12: Sc2tog twice, sc until the last 4 sts, sc2tog twice. Ch1, turn. (26)

Rows 13–16: Sc2tog, sc until last 2 sts, sc2tog. Ch1, turn. (18)

Row 17 and 18: Sc2tog twice, sc until the last 4 sts, sc2tog twice. Ch1, turn. (10)

Row 19: Sl st 4 times, switch to red yarn, and begin the cherry.

Row 20: Ch 12, sl st into the next open st in the frosting. Ch1, turn. (12)

Row 21: Hdc into each st. Sl st back into the frosting. Tie off, and bury the ends of the yarn.

Repeat with all four cake pieces.

Sew two sides together using a whipstitch around the edges, and block flat.

Danette

Location: Santa Monica, California

Reason You Went Vegan: Six years ago, after I drove my business into the ground, I went on an epic eating binge from Thanksgiving to Epiphany. I called it the Holiday Gorge. After, I felt sick, gross, bloated, and barely likable. I decided to try veganism for a month, to feel better health-wise. During that time, I read extensively about how being a vegan could nullify my contribution to the most destructive industries and practices. I didn't look back. That month will easily extend to a lifetime. Being vegan has had a very positive influence on me and my surroundings—more than any other single decision I've made.

Favorite Dish to Cook: The family's version of rice and beans, Puerto Rican style; 90 percent of the time, this dish is traditionally prepared vegan anyway. This dish is a staple in my home, whether to impress, to comfort, or to celebrate. I can never go wrong with rice and beans.

Funniest Vegan Moment: One summer, while visiting my husband's grandmother in Puerto Rico, she made a soup and assured me that there was no meat or dairy in it. After a couple spoonfuls, a pink cube floated to the top. It was a chunk of ham. "For flavor!" she said. Although I've been vegan for six years, I haven't eaten meat for nearly thirty. I nearly fainted off the chair! The recurring image of that floating pink cube haunts me still.

ART CREDITS

Illustrations by Michelle Cavigliano, www.myzoetrope.com

Photography by:

- Hannah Kaminsky, www.bittersweetblog.com
- Nicole Carpenter, www.nicoleleephoto.com/blog
- Patrick Rafanan, www.soybaby.com
- Jeanine Michelle, www.jeaninemichelle.net

Photos also provided by Chris Marco, Ama Lea, City Down, Celine Steen, Matt Miller, Kip Dorrell, Jenn Shagrin, Bianca Phillips, and George Sierzputowski.

Tyler Steer and Melisser at the Farm Sanctuary Hoe Down 2008

ACKNOWLEDGMENTS

Writing this book was a new experience for me, and I couldn't have done it without a cast of supportive people who helped along the way. The outpouring of support has been overwhelming and heartwarming, and I can't even begin to thank you all!

Ryan, you are always there for me—whether it's lending an ear or being force-fed my creations, I know I can count on you. I love you and our furry family with all of my heart, and I'm thankful for that San Francisco night in 1998. Mooks por vida!

To my recipe testers who kept it real and made sure the food in this book was worthy of your time. You rule at life! Alyssa Franchetti, Carmen Borsa, Constanze Reichardt, Emma Clarke, Gabrielle Pope, Honor Fabun, Jennifer McVea, Jessica Olson, Laura Pope, Megan McClellan, Melissa Gray, and Nicole Carpenter.

Bianca, Celine, Constanze, Crystal, Hannah, Jenn, Julie, Kelly, Kip, Kittee, Terry, and the Sugar Beat Sweets ladybros, you seriously rocked my world with your culinary prowess. My book is 100 times better because of you all!

Adriana, City, Erika, Gena, Kristen, Natala, and Sunny—thank you for sharing your knowledge and expertise for the book. I can't think of a better pack of ladies to be involved!

Alice, Allison, Blythe, Danielle, Elizabeth, Emiko, Erika, Jen, Jeanette, Karla, Kerry, Leanne, Leigh, Michelle, Rithika, Sara, Secret Supper, and Tracy—your businesses make the world a better place, and I am grateful for you all!

Alyssa, Bahar, Carmen, Cassandra, Christine, Danette, Ditte, Glauce, Jess, Jojo, Laura, Laviyah, Luciana, Marijke, Marika, Mel, Melanie F., Melanie P., Monique, Roberta, Silvia, Teenuja—thank you for letting me pick your brains about vegan life; you're all great examples for veganism, and a pack of lookers!

Hannah, thank you for the amazing photographs! The days we spent together were so much fun, and I love your vision and photography style. You also rock at recipes and crafts; how do you do it?!

Nicole, the "ladies who lunch" photo shoot was mayhem, but a total blast. Thank you for taking on last-minute assignments and saving my ass!

Michelle, my book is properly adorable thanks to your artwork. My heart melts every time I see the Strummer drawing. I'm so glad you allowed me to share your talents with others.

Gabrielle, in my moments of insanity, you reined it all in, gave me confidence, and taught me how to be a better writer. Can you edit my blog next?

Isa and Terry, needless to say, I love your books, but I really love *you*. Thank you for answering my silly questions and guiding me in the right direction, on top of being awesome friends. I'm so happy to have met you both.

Mom, Dad, Jeanette, and Kyle, thank you for letting me march to my own drummer, and for putting up with it. Every vegan meal you eat means the world to me.

Grandma, I appreciate the love for all things vintage that you instilled in me, and I think it's safe to say you're the coolest grandma on Facebook!

To my ladybros all around the world: San Francisco, Chicago, NYC, LA, Vienna, Brighton, Hamburg, and everywhere in between! Thank you for showing me I don't have to hang out with all dudes; lady friends are where it's at!

Thank you, Skyhorse Publishing, for taking a chance on me, and for allowing me to fulfill my dreams.

To everyone who tweeted, re-tweeted, blogged, posted on Facebook, and lent me words of encouragement, THANK YOU! Yes, only a true nerd would thank the Internet. No shame!

To all vegans everywhere—keep fighting the good fight, and thank you for making the world a better place.